ASTRA ZERO

Dark Vintage

COLLECTION

VOL. 2

**A DARK AND SEXY COLLECTION OF ART
INSPIRED BY MIXING AND REVAMPING OLD HISTORICAL ARTWORK
WITH A MORE EROTIC, MUSCULAR MALE BODY DRIVEN AND
SOMETIMES HORROR THEMED LENS**

BY GAY ALTERNATIVE CANADIAN ARTIST: ASTRA ZERO

THIS BOOK IS MADE FOR ADULTS ONLY 18+

astrazero.com  @astrazero

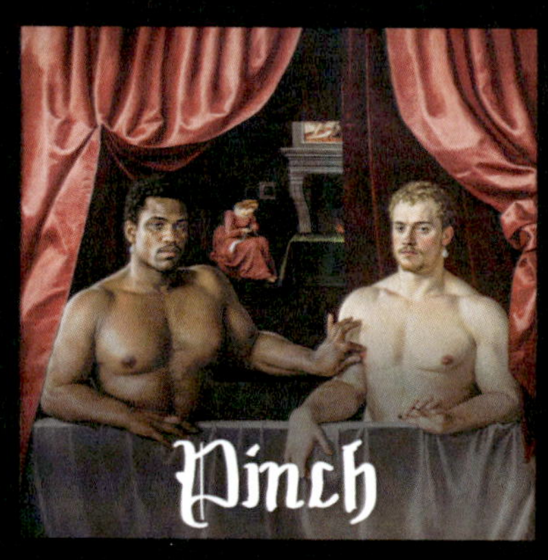

ASTRA ZERO REVAMP OF, PORTRAIT
PRESUME DE GABRIELLE D'ESTREES ET DE
SA SOEUR LA DUCHESSE DE VILLARS, BY
UNKNOWN ARTIST FROM THE SCHOOL OF
FONTAINEBLEAU , 1594

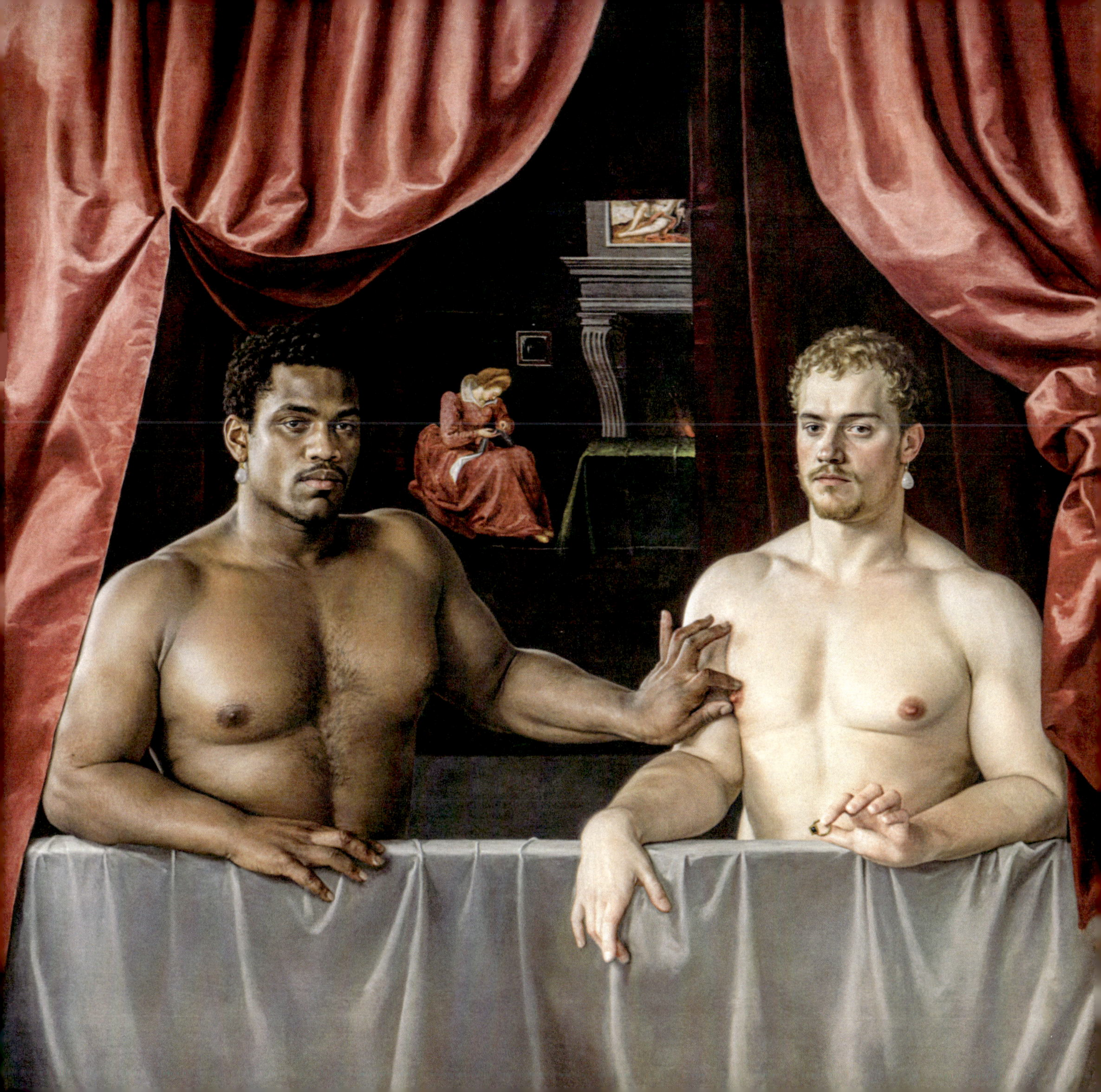

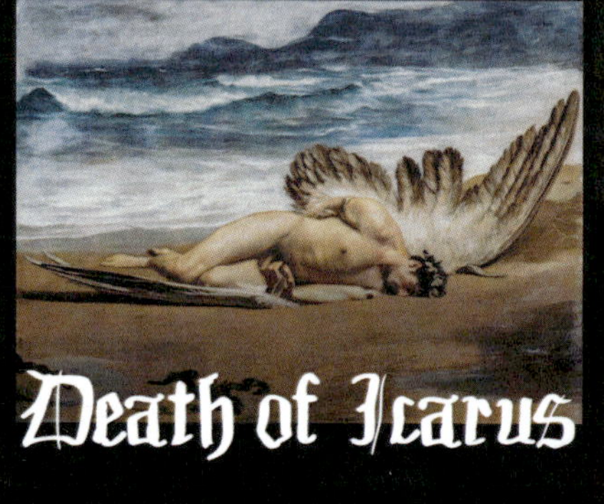

ASTRA ZERO REVAMP OF,
THE DEATH OF ICARUS,
BY ALEXANDRE CABANEL,
1823-1889

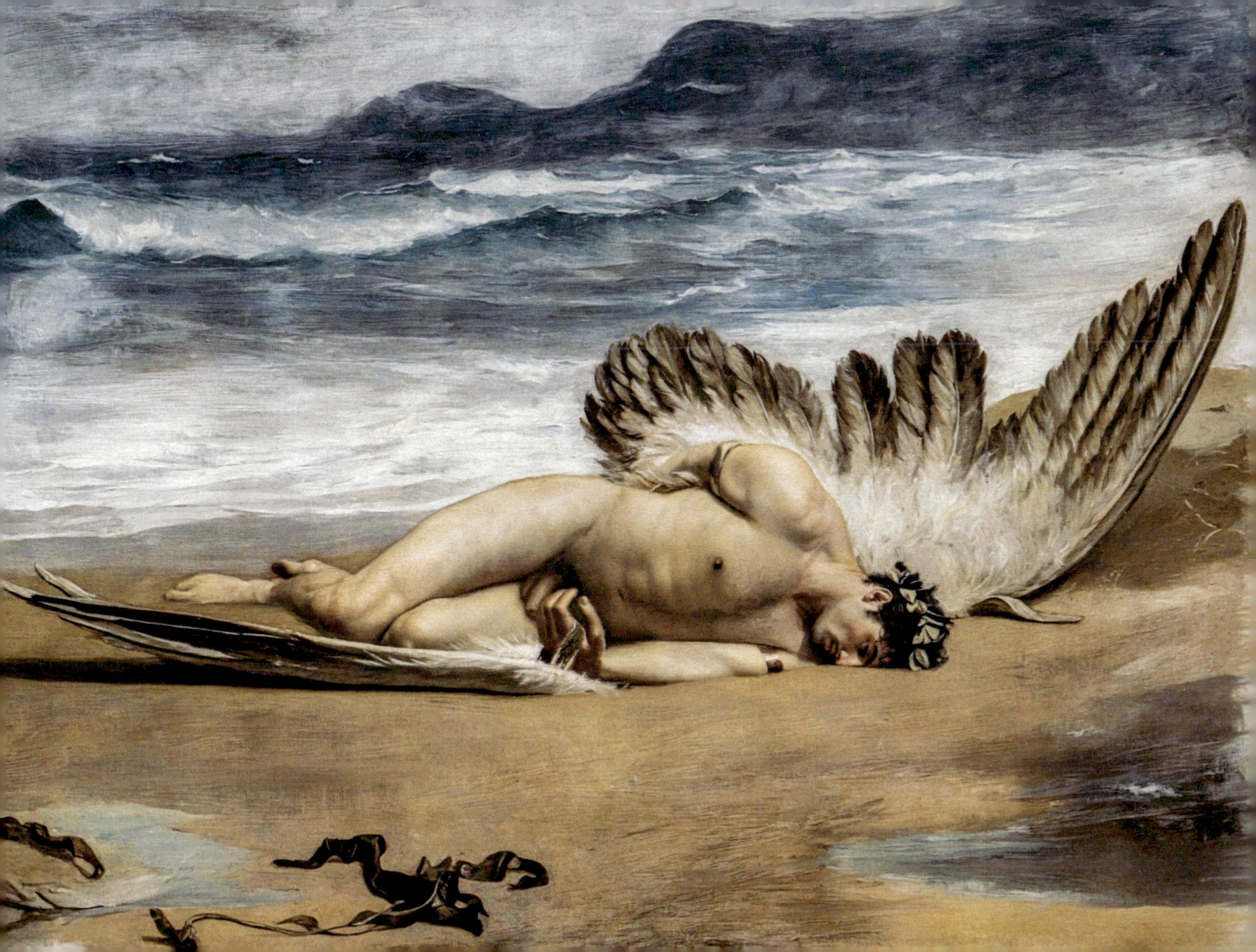

Reaching for the moon

ASTRA ZERO REVAMP OF,
REACHING FOR THE MOON,
BY EDWARD MASON EGGLESTON,
1933

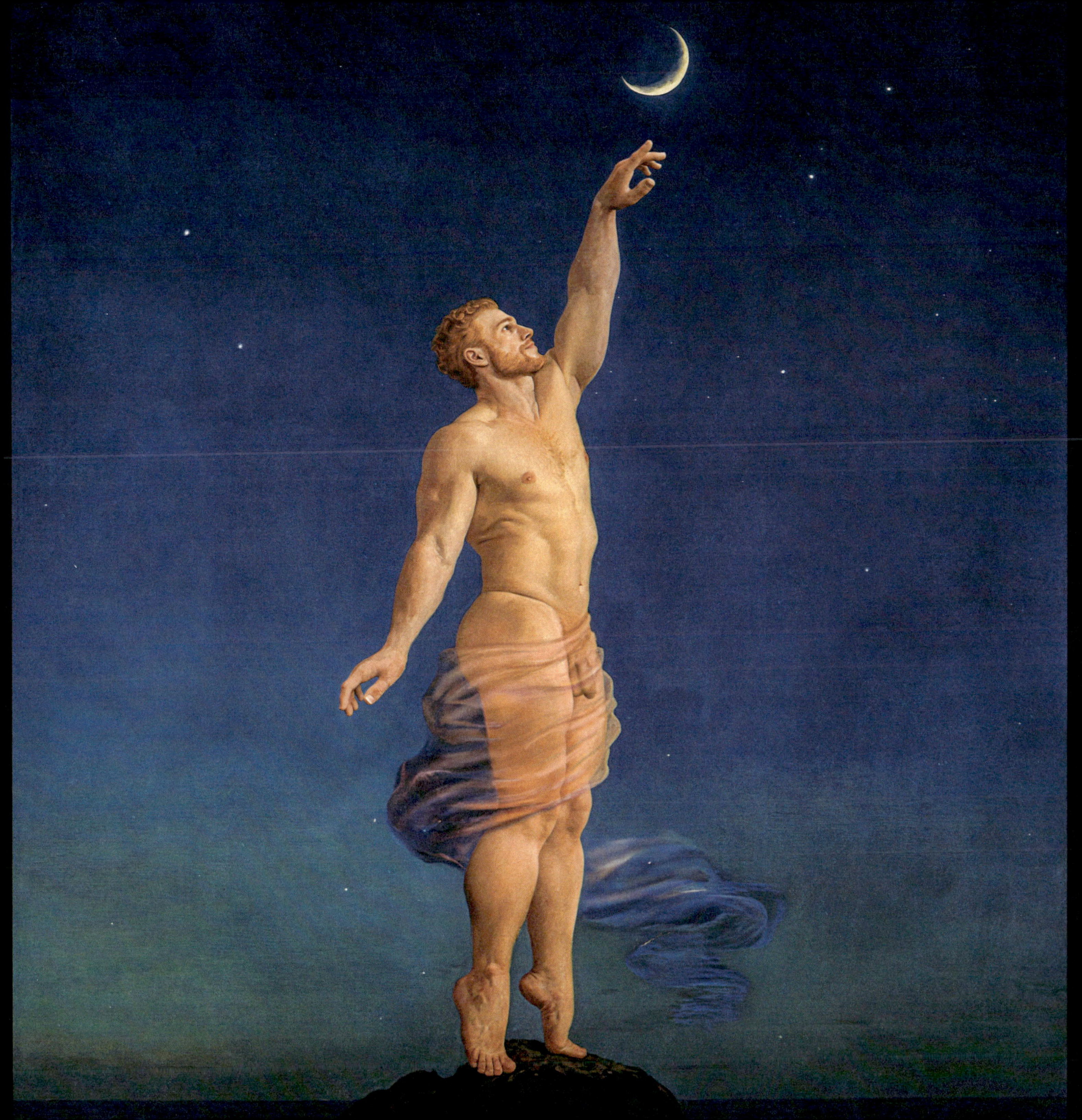

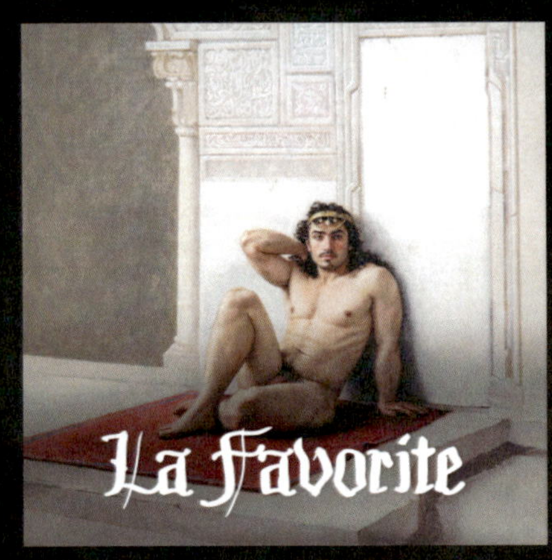

ASTRA ZERO REVAMP OF,
LA FAVORITE,
BY LUIS RICARDO FALERO,
AROUND 1866

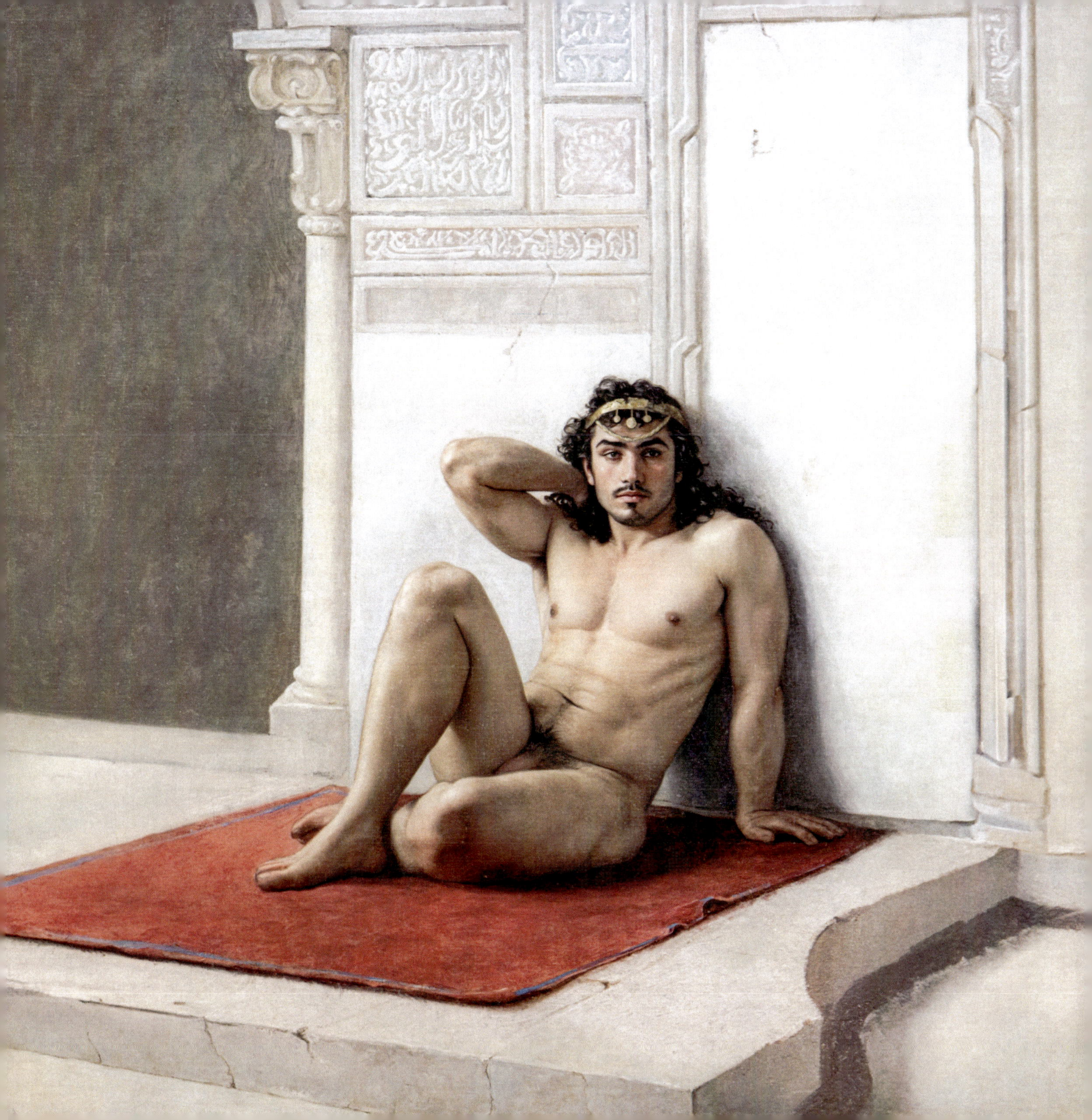

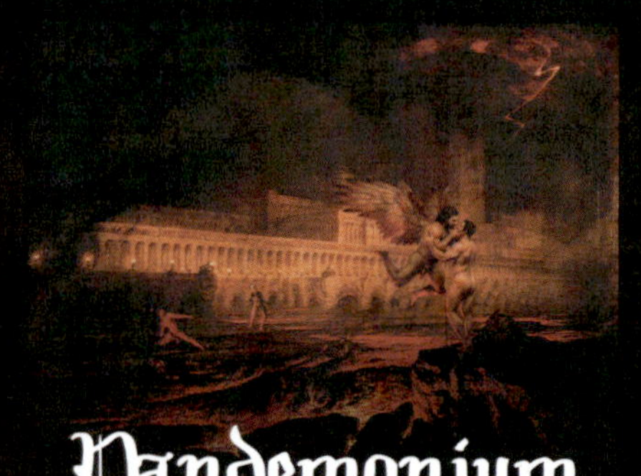

Pandemonium

ASTRA ZERO REVAMP OF,
PANDEMONIUM,
BY JOHN MARTIN,
1841

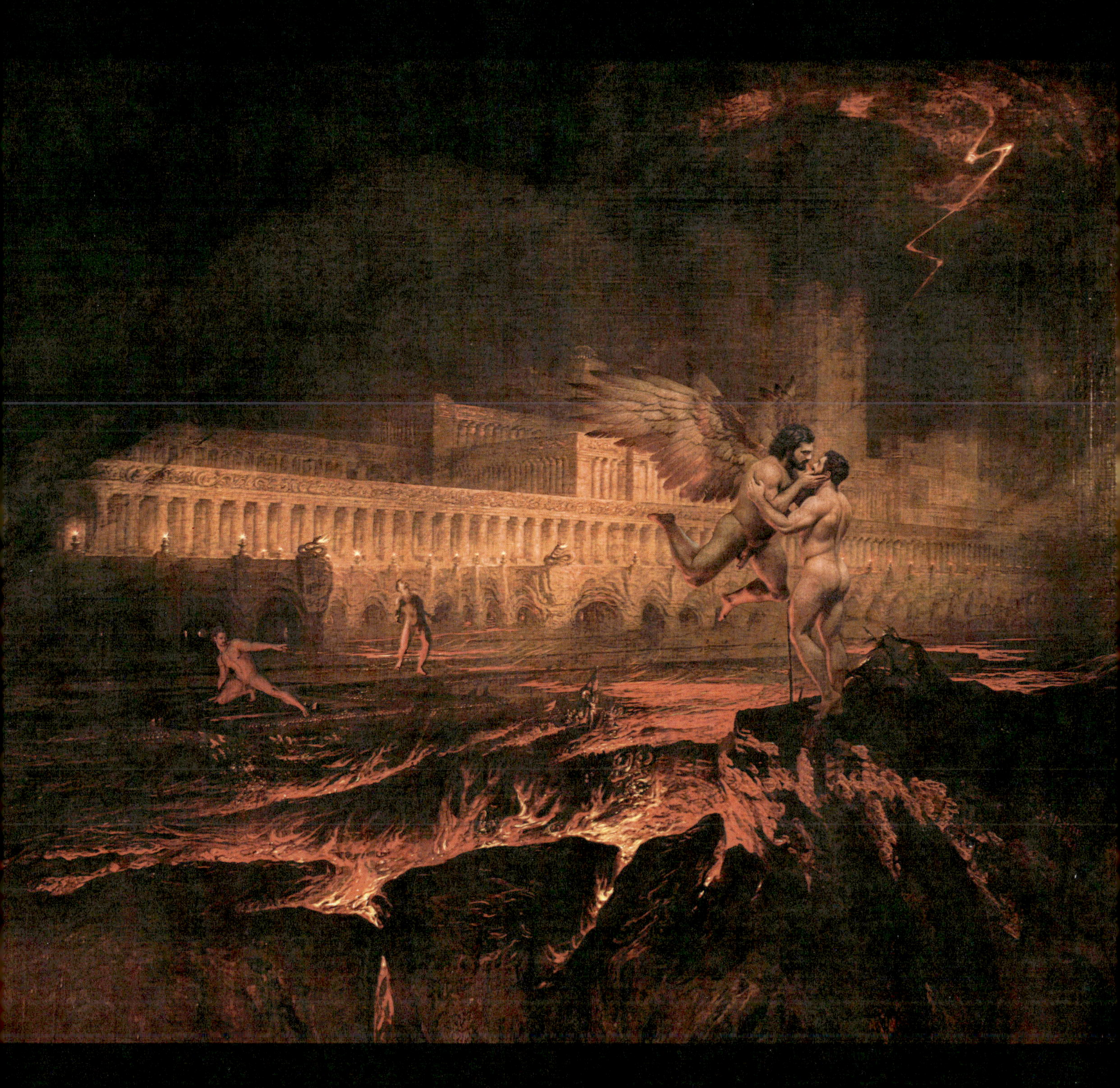

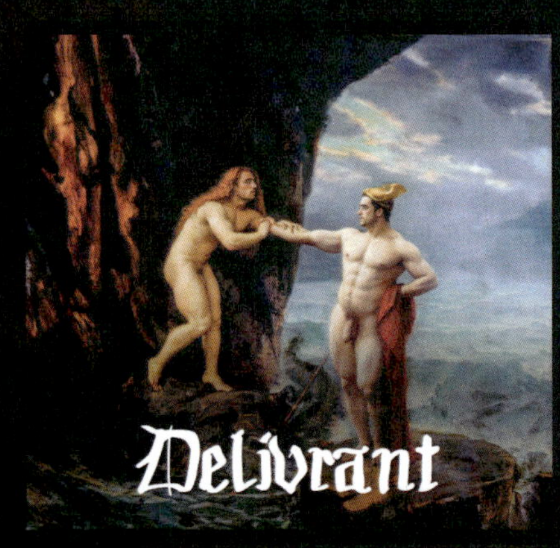

ASTRA ZERO SLIGHT REVAMP OF,
PERSEE DELIVRANT ANDROMEDE,
BY GUSTAVE COURTOIS, 1913

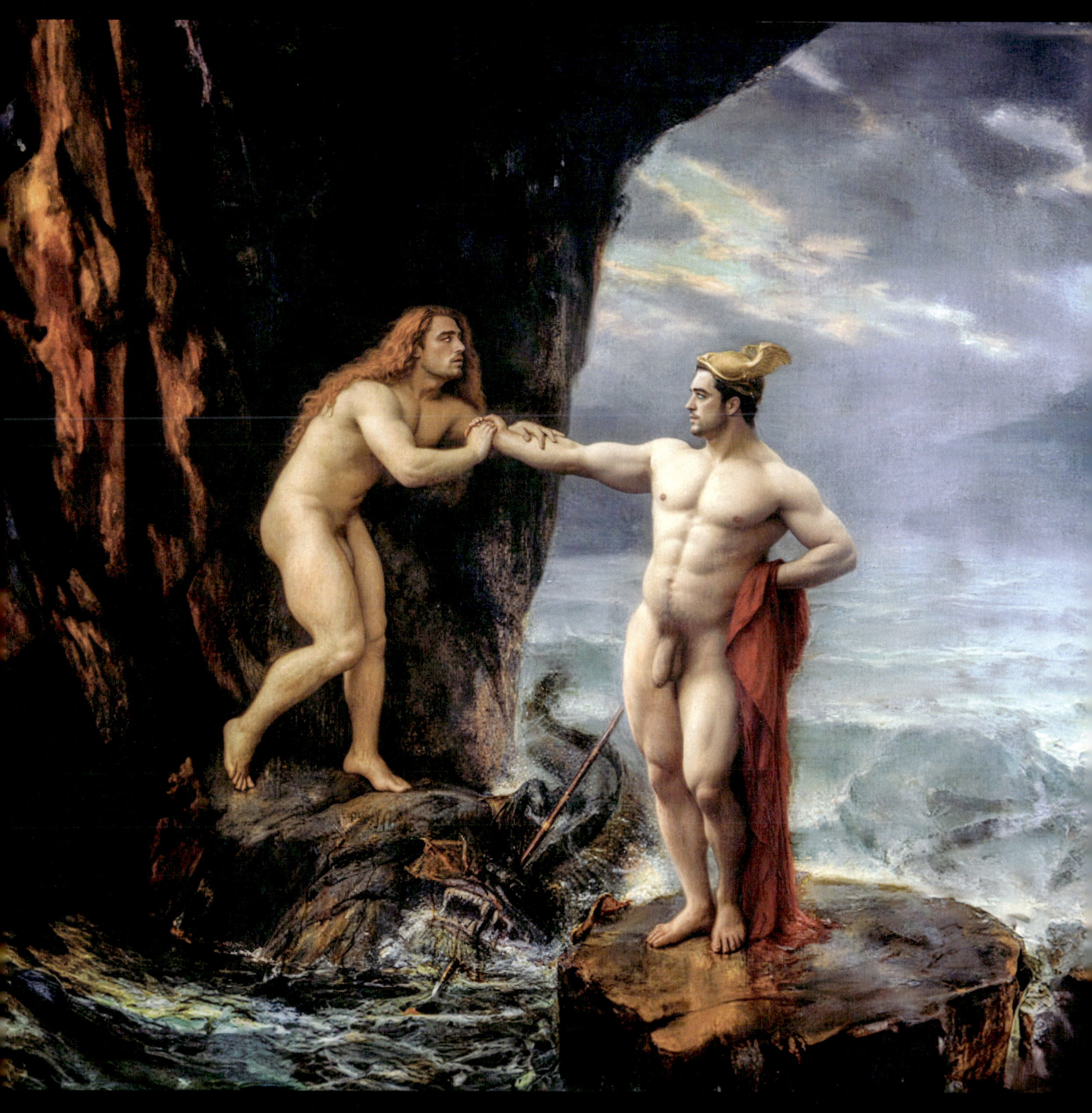

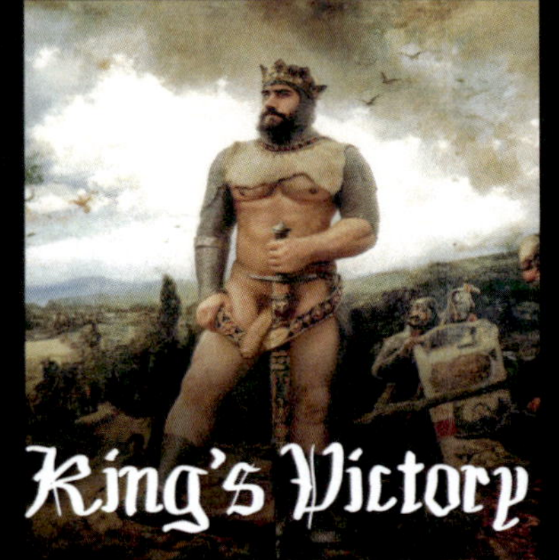

ASTRA ZERO REVAMP OF,
ALFONSO I DE ARAGON,
BY FRANCISCO PRADILLA ORTI
1879

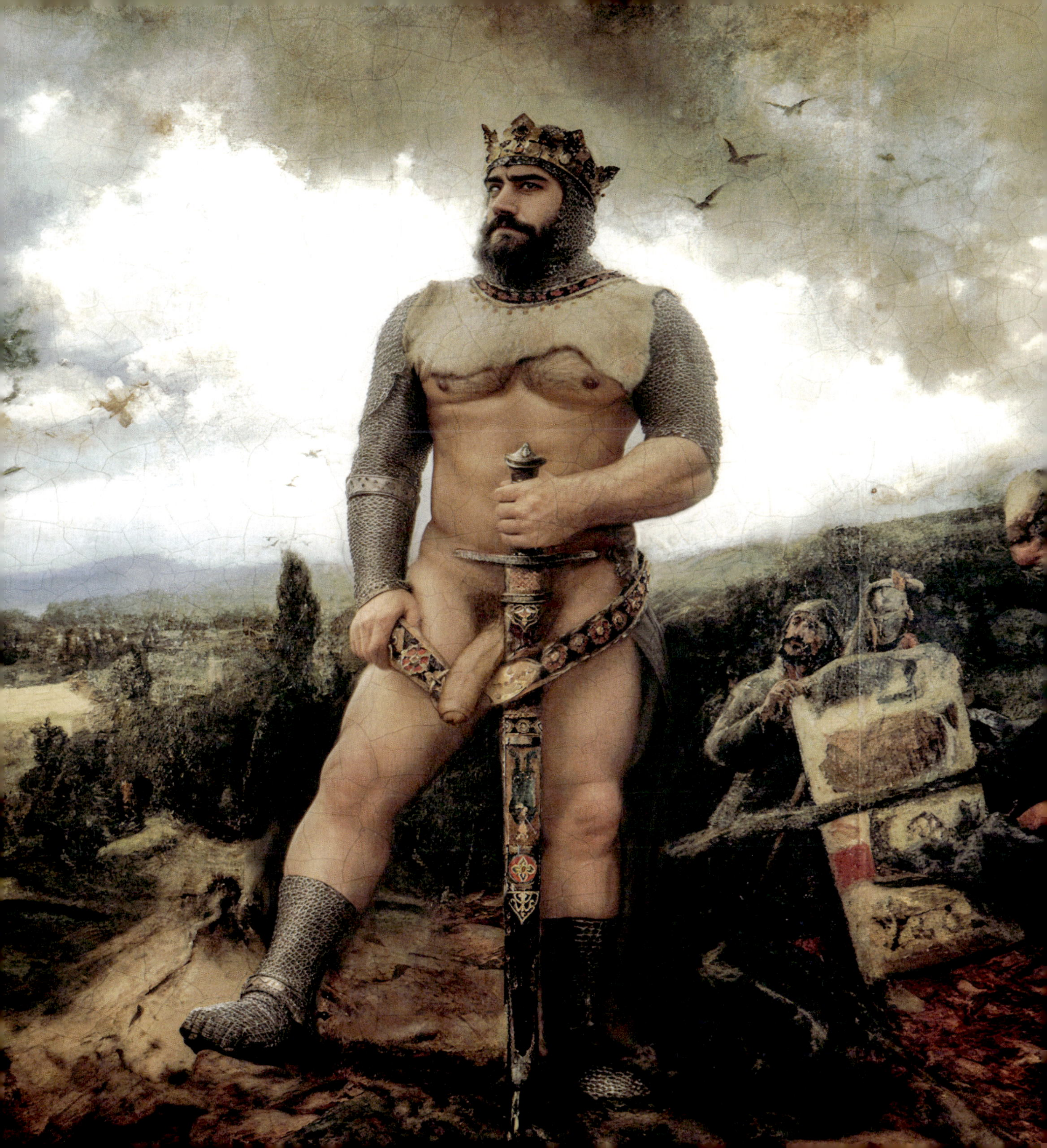

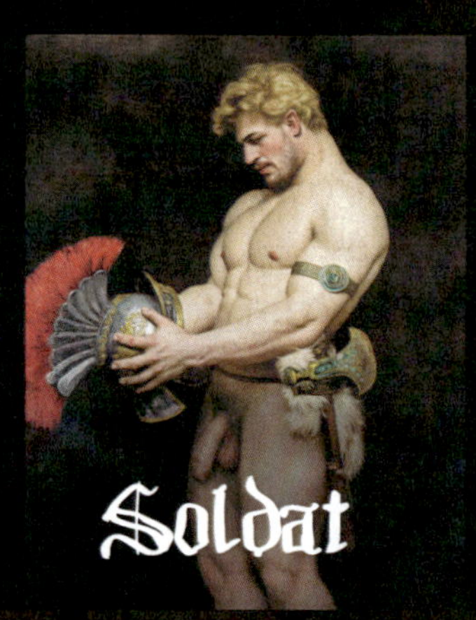

ASTRA ZERO REVAMP OF,
SOLDAT GERMAIN AVEC UN CASQUE,
BY OSMAR SCHINDLER, 1902

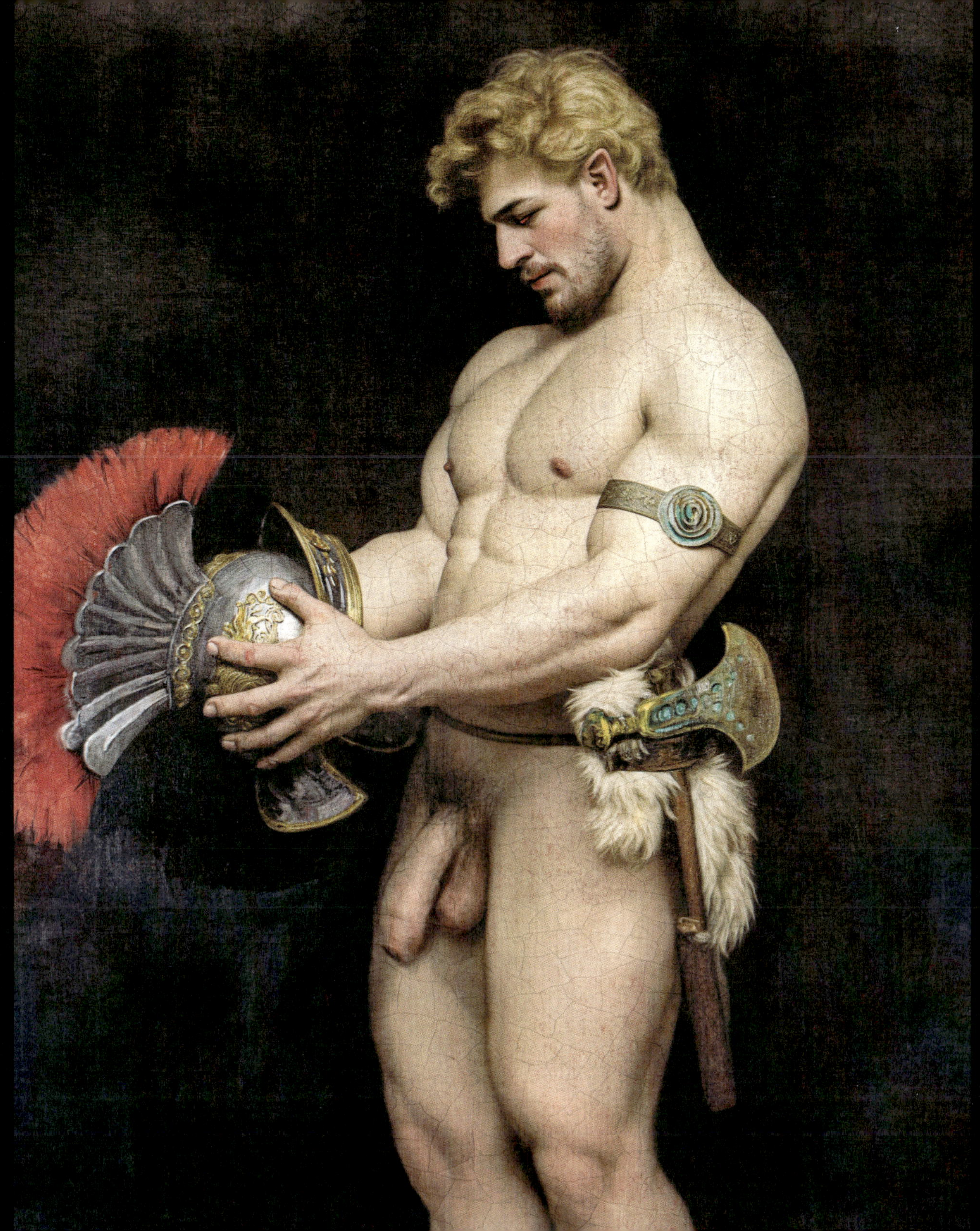

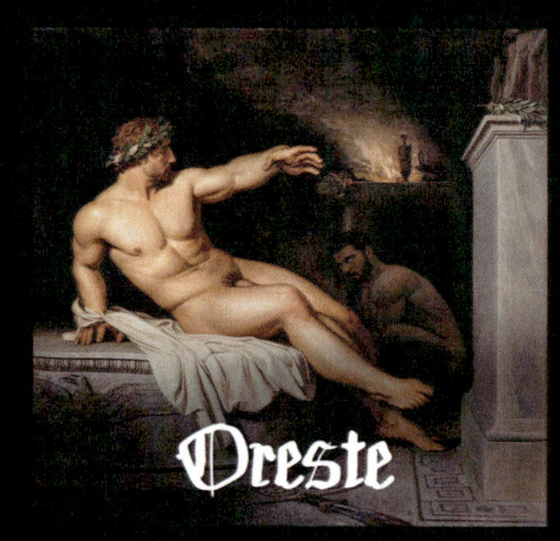# Oreste

ASTRA ZERO REVAMP OF,
ORESTE, BY ALEXANDRE CABANEL,
1846

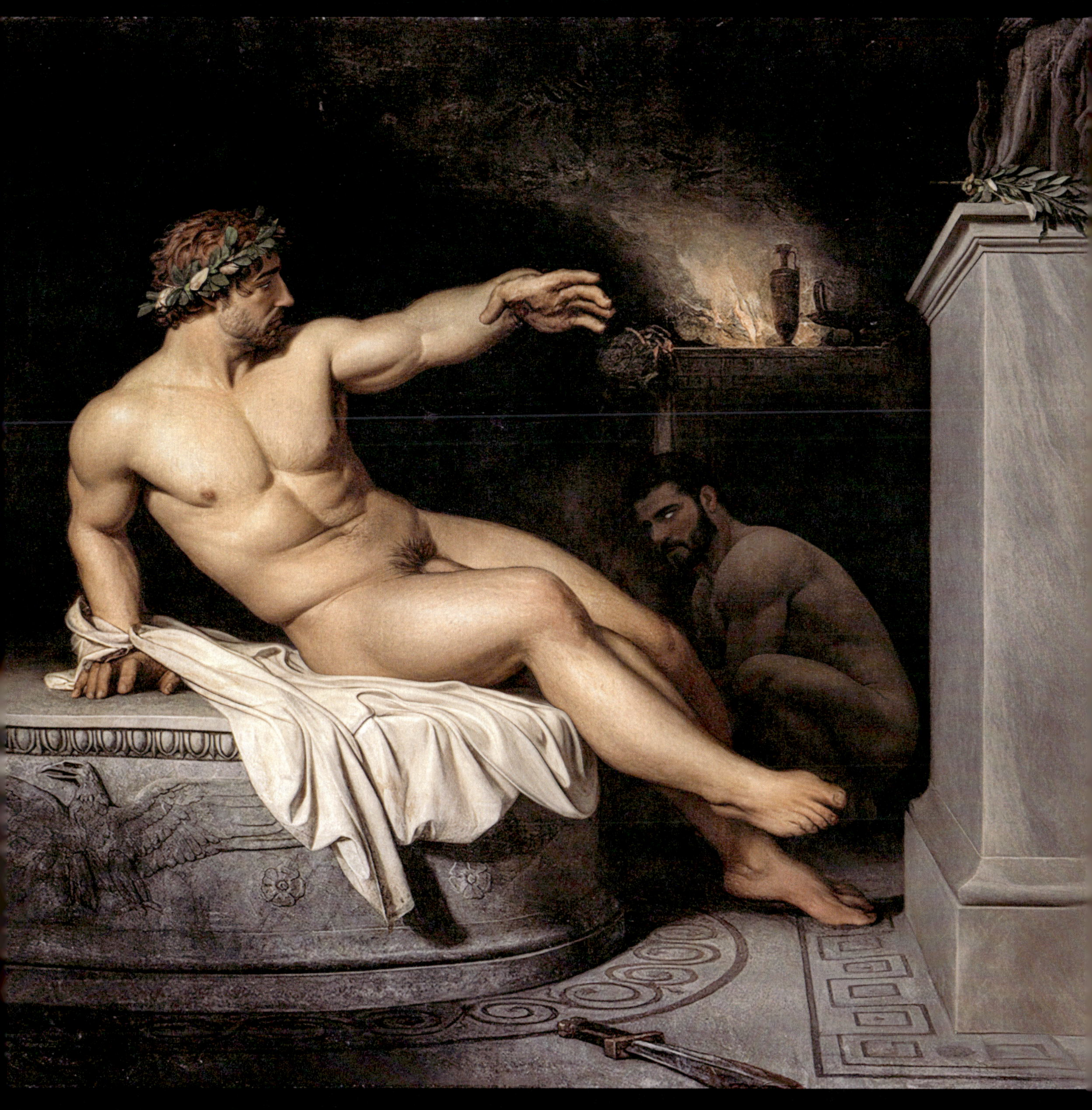

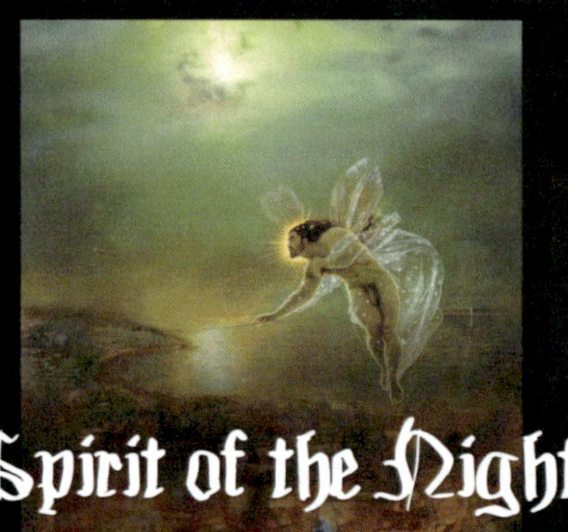

Spirit of the Night

ASTRA ZERO SLIGHT REVAMP OF,
SPIRIT OF THE NIGHT
BY JOHN ATKINSON GRIMSHAW,
1879

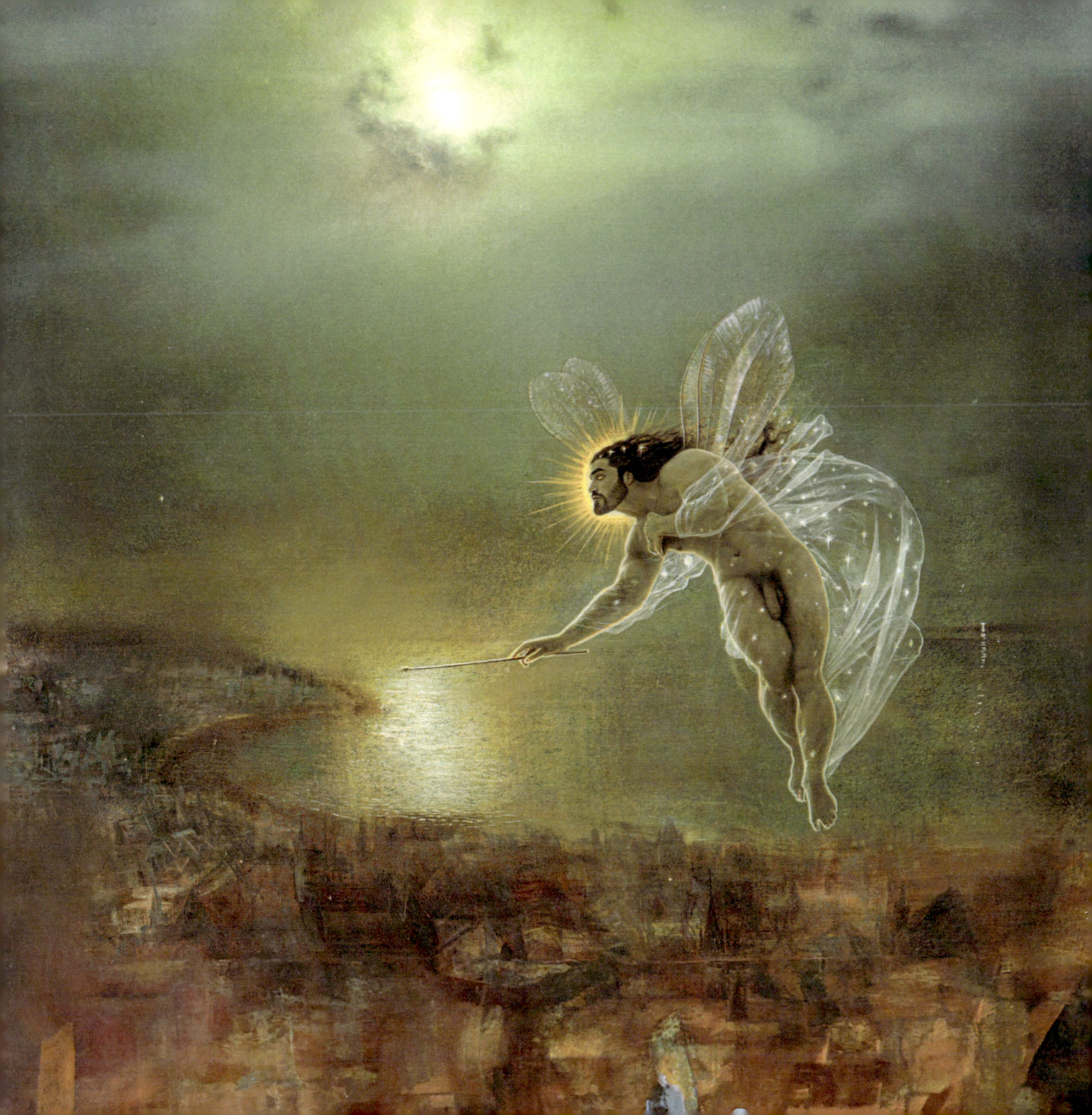

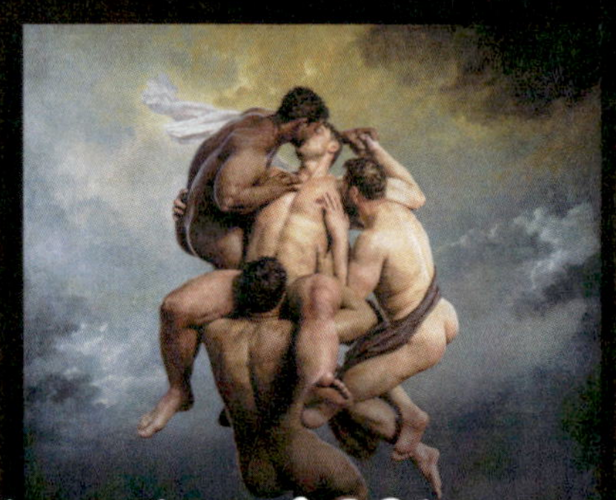

Angels of Pleasure

ASTRA ZERO REVAMP OF,
LA FEMME DAMNEE,
BY OCTAVE TASSAERT,
1859

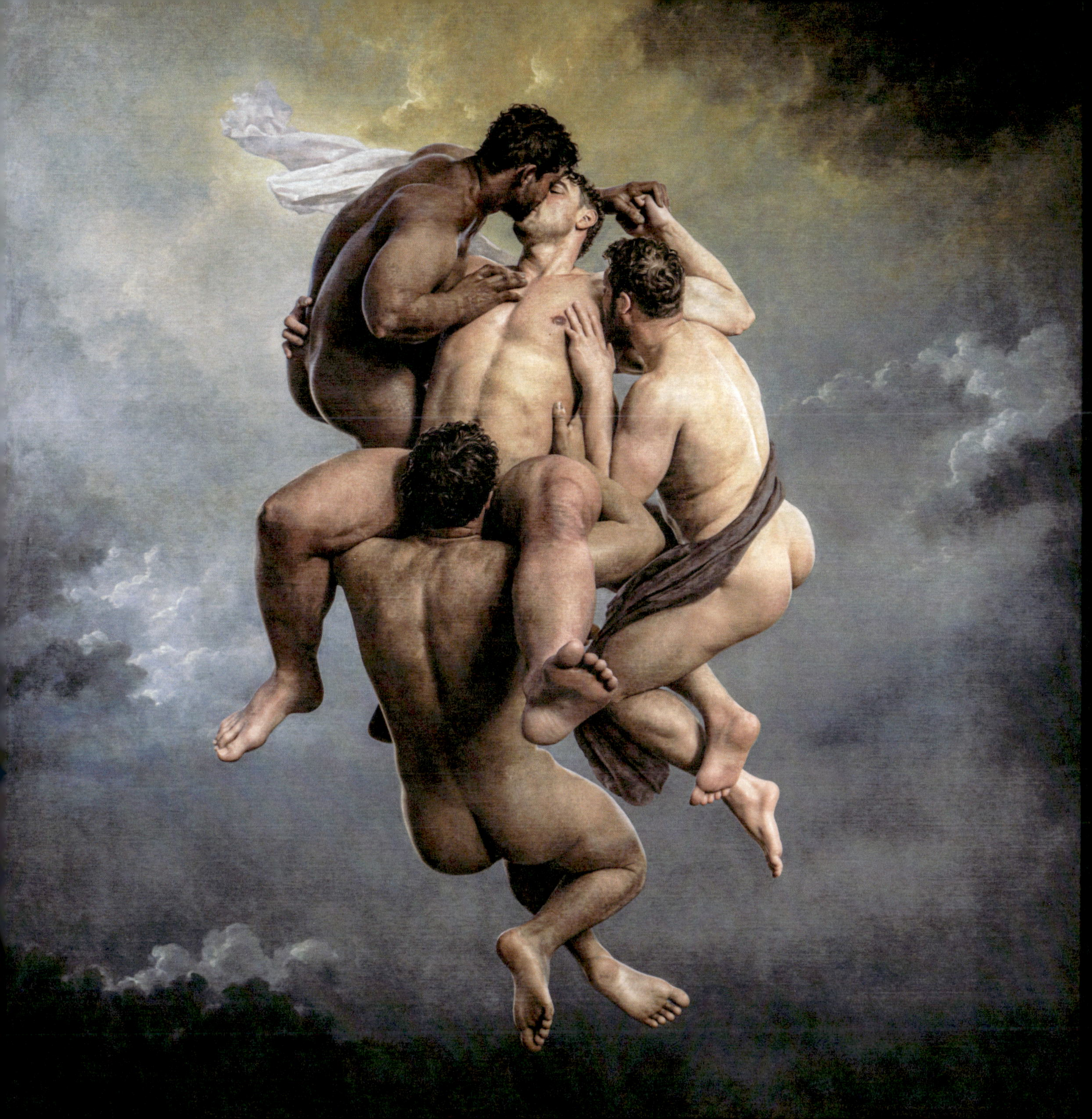

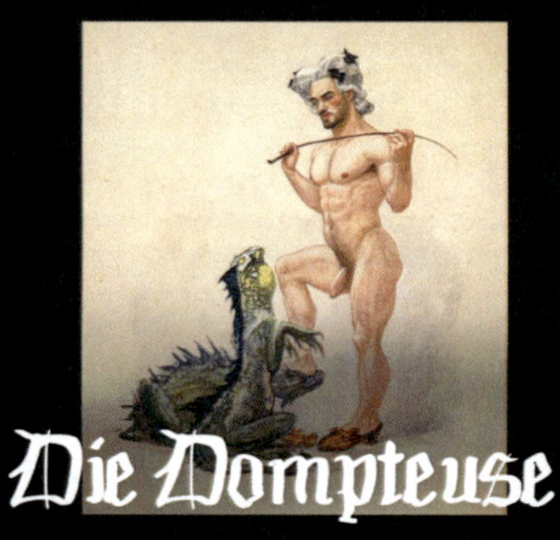

ASTRA ZERO REVAMP OF,
DIE DOMPTEUSE,
BY HEINRICH KLEY,
1910

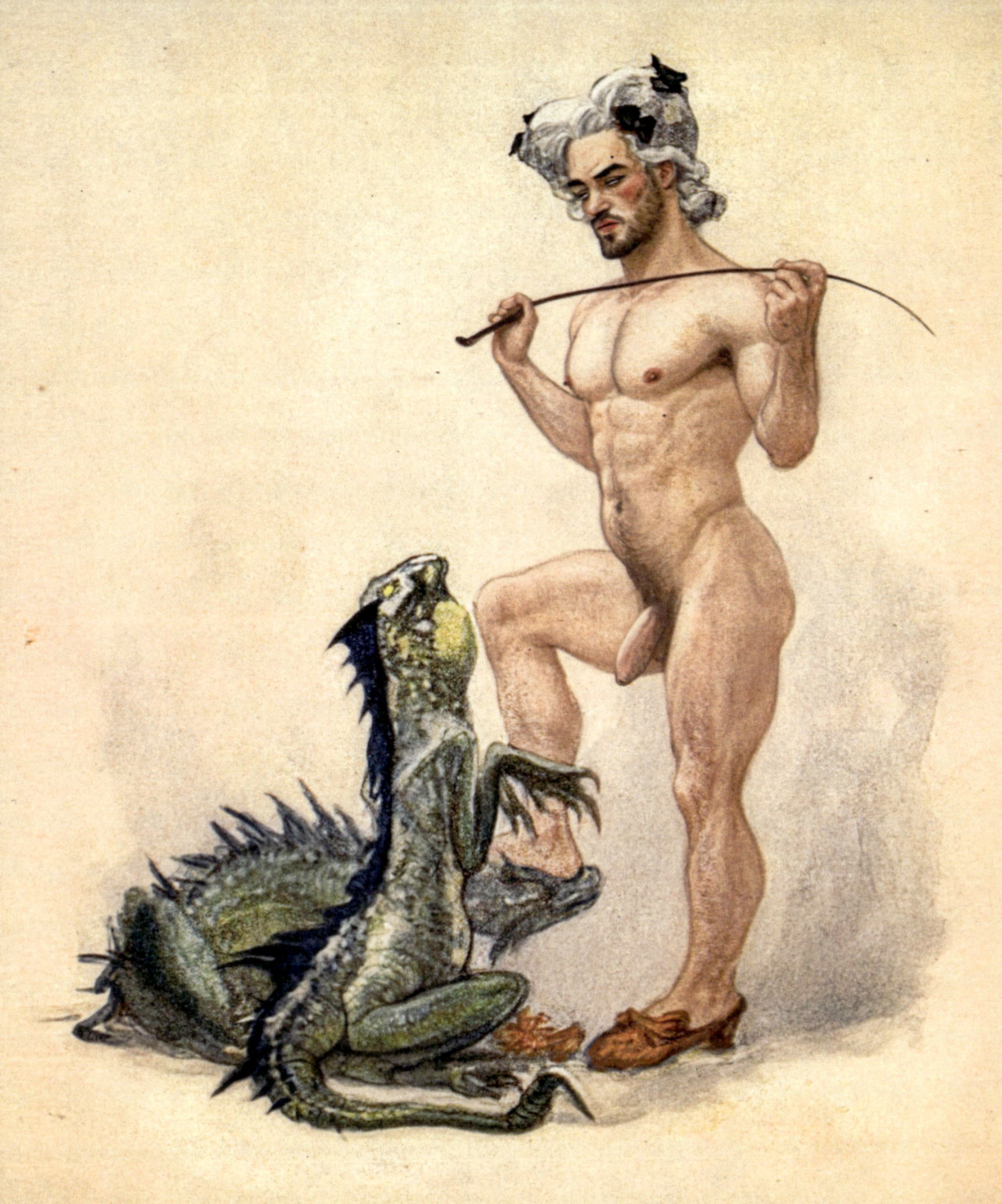

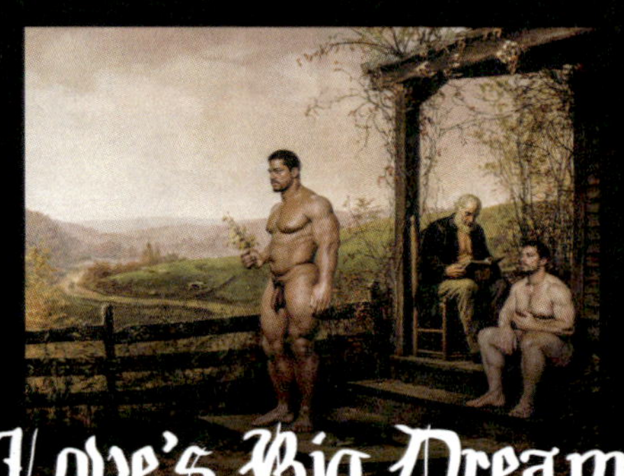

Love's Big Dream

ASTRA ZERO REVAMP OF,
LOVE'S YOUNG DREAM,
BY JENNIE AUGUSTA BROWNSCOMBE,
1887

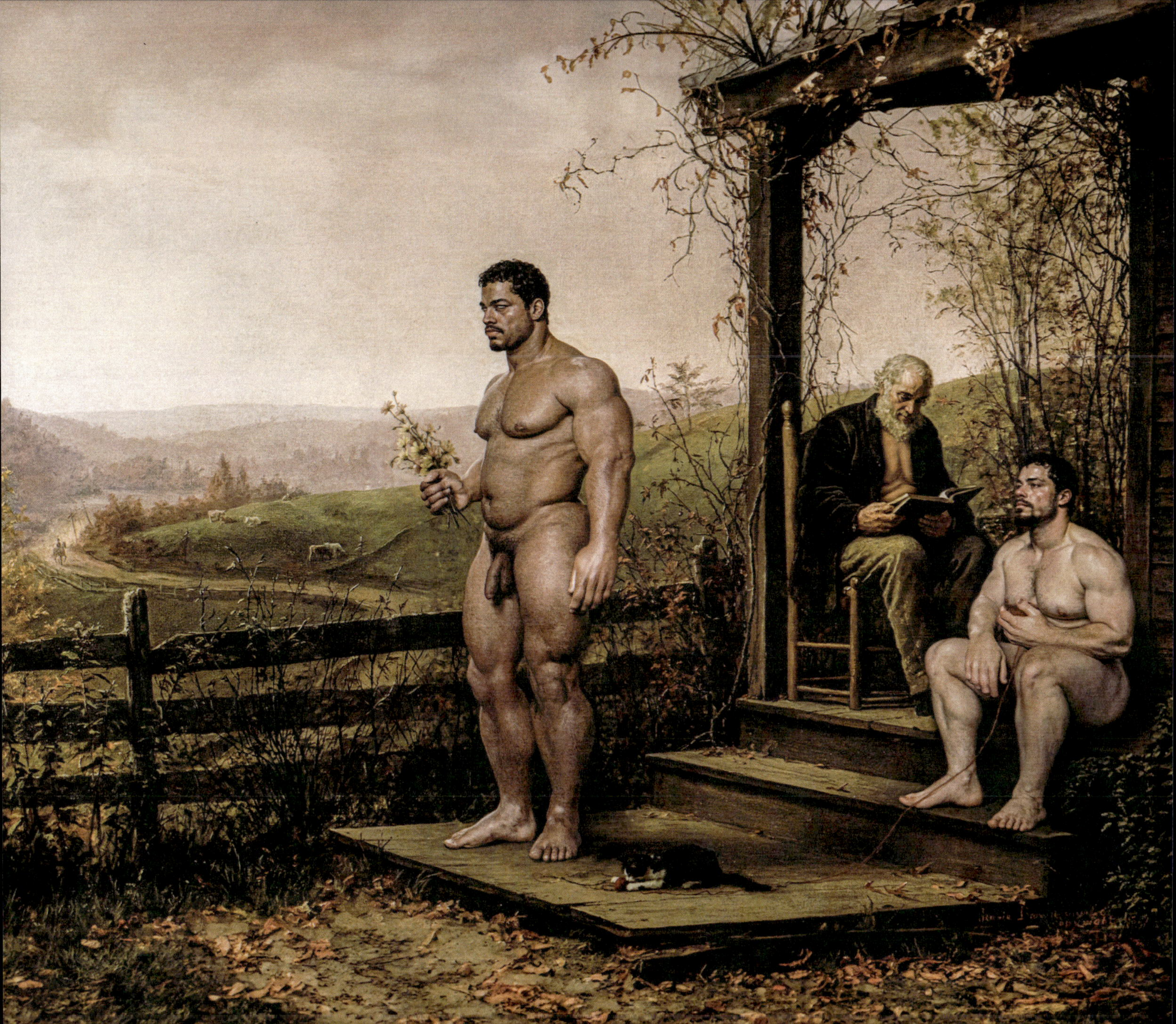

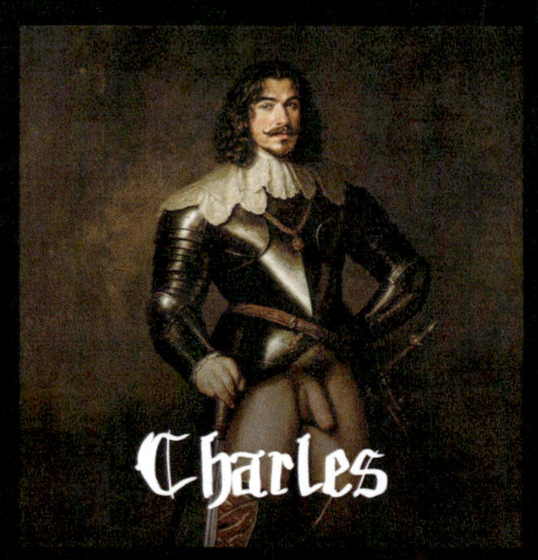

ASTRA ZERO REVAMP OF,
CHARLES LOUIS,
BY ANTHONY VAN DYCK,
1637

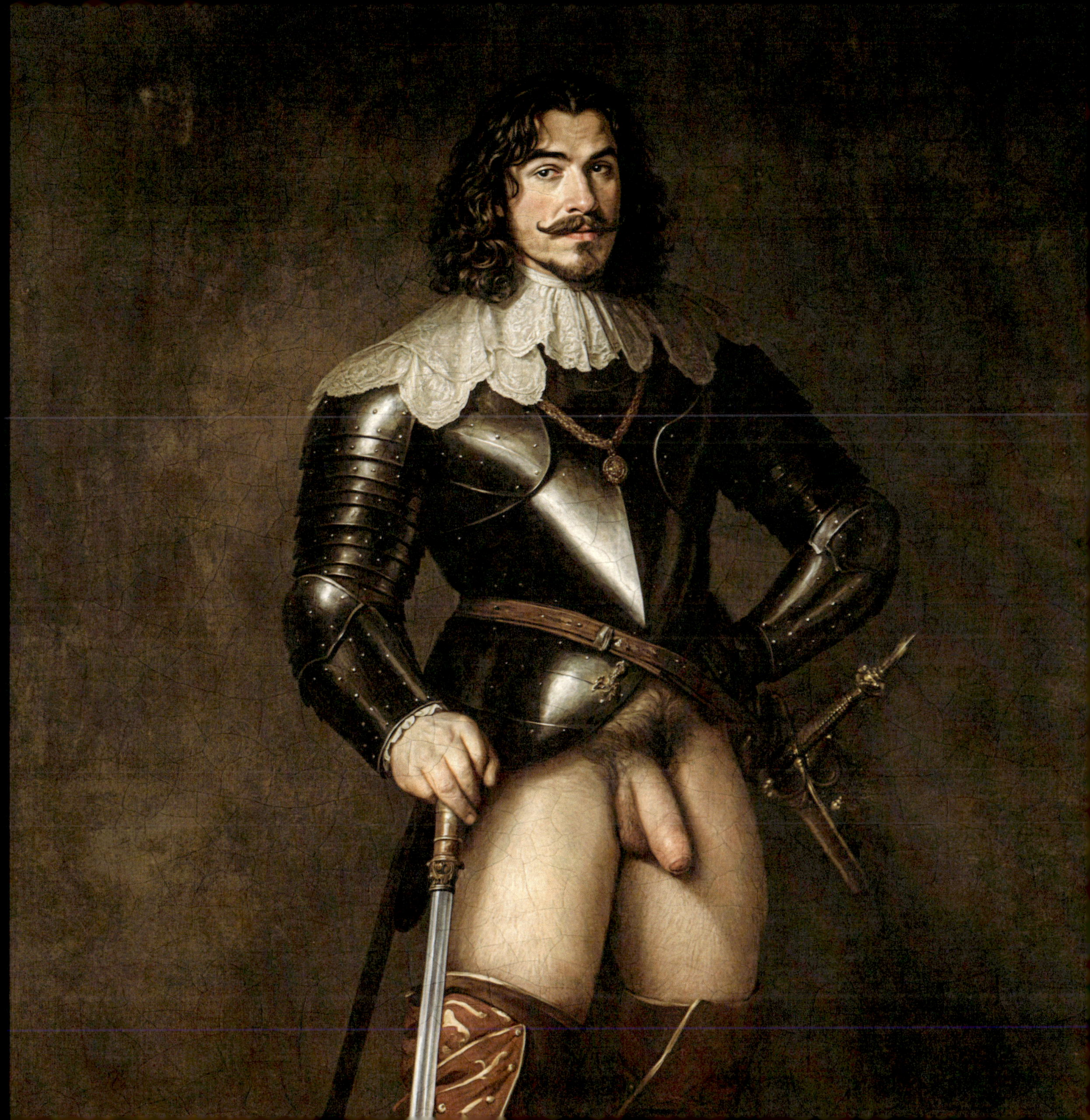

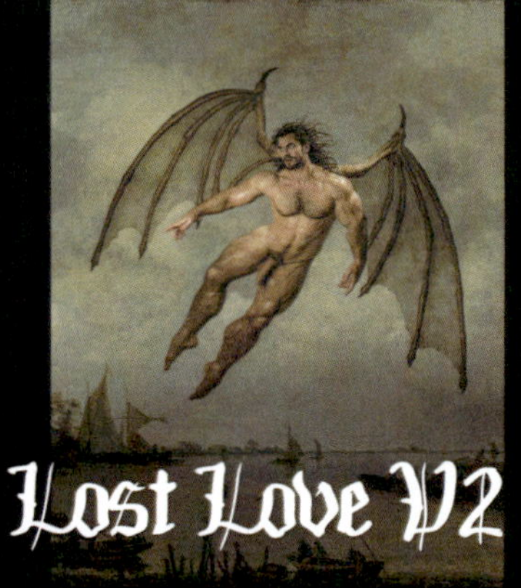

ASTRA ZERO MIXED MEDIA PAINTING,
BACKGROUND INSPIRED BY UNKNOWN
WORK FROM THE 1600S

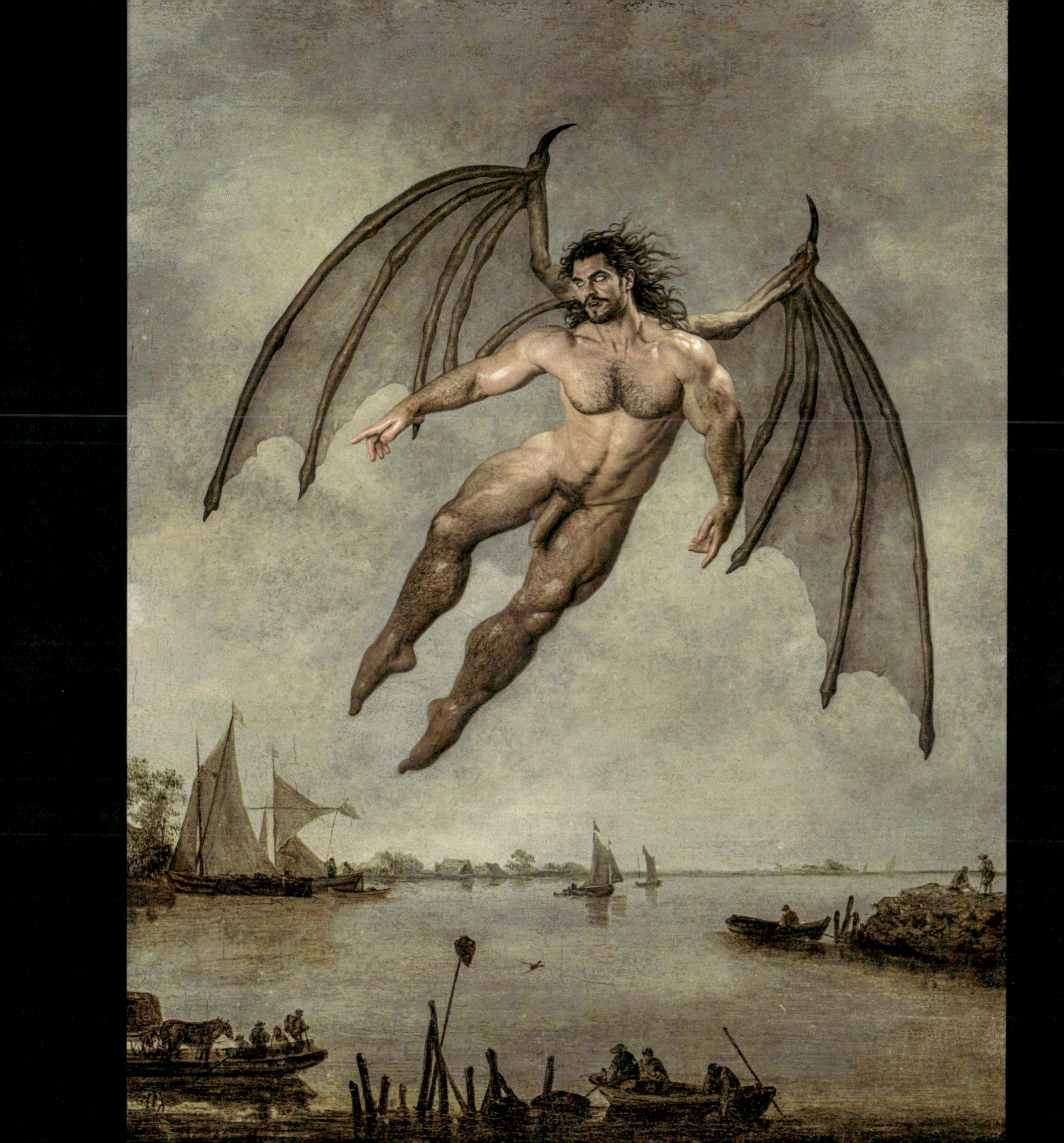

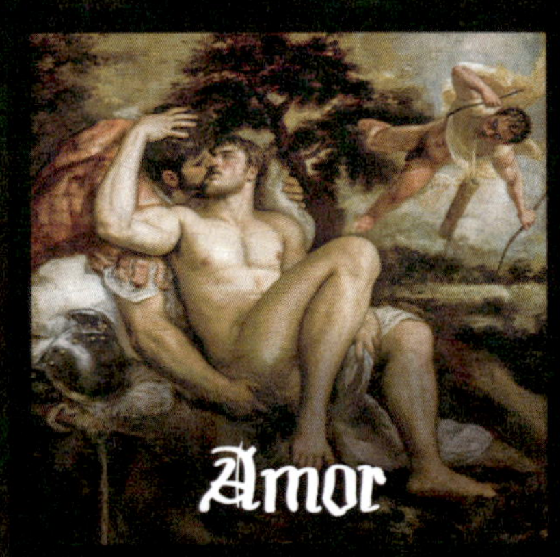

ASTRA ZERO REVAMP OF,
MARS, VENUS UND AMOR,
BY TITIAN, 1530

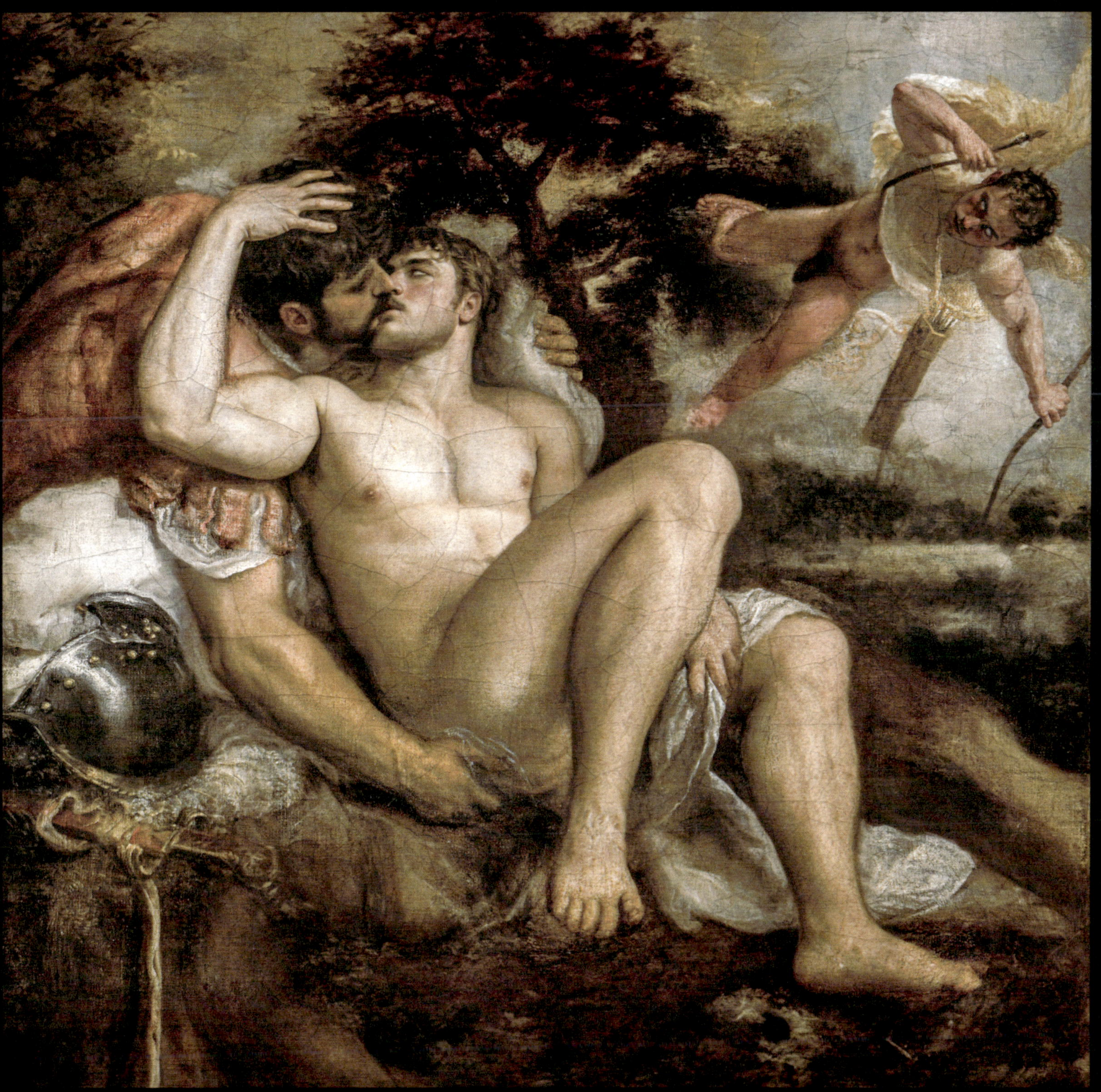

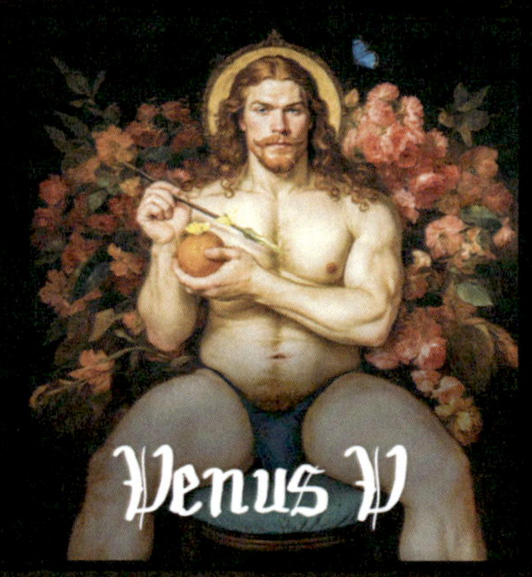

ASTRA ZERO REVAMP OF,
VENUS VERTICORDIA,
BY DANTE GABRIEL ROSSETTI,
1864

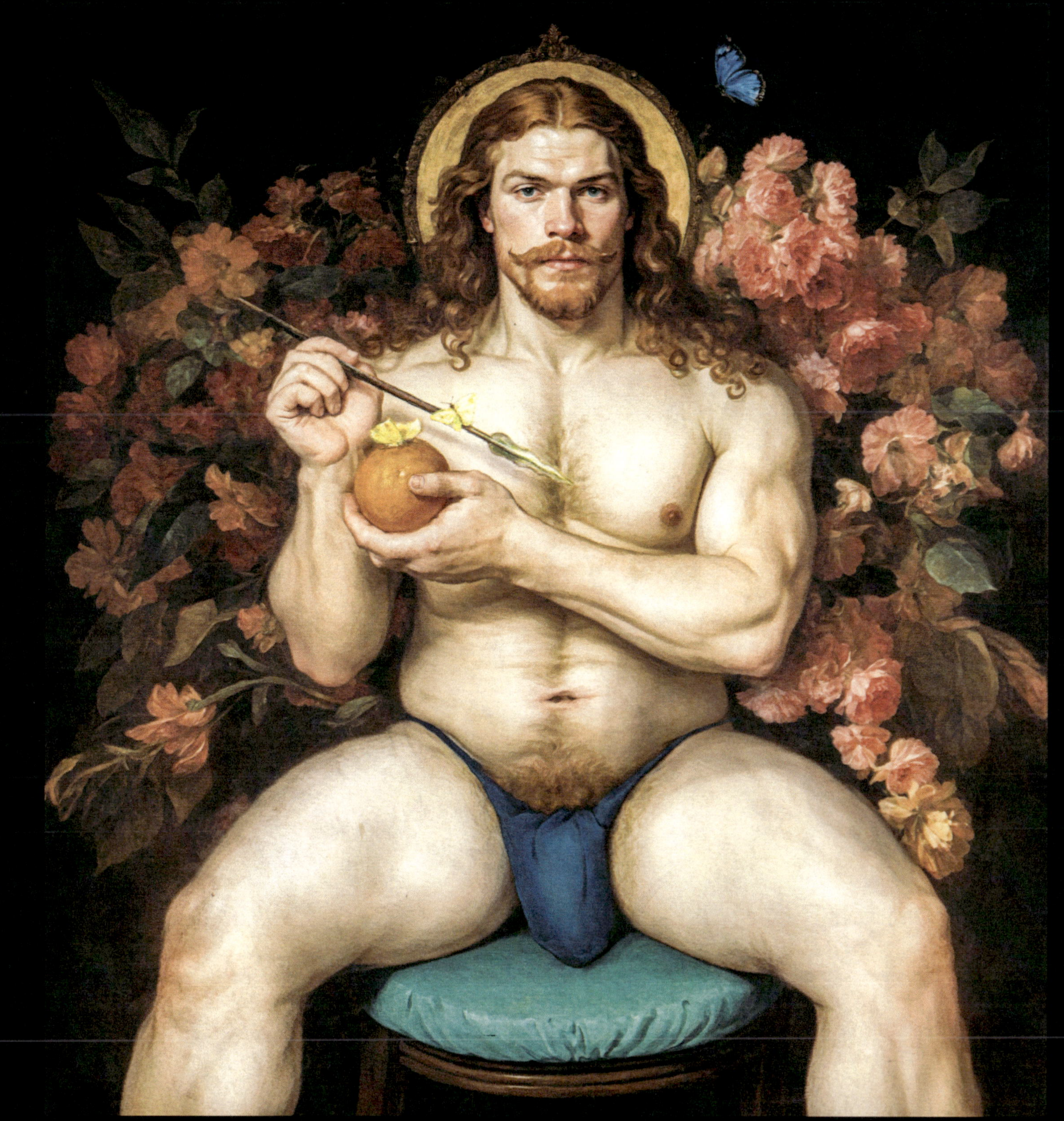

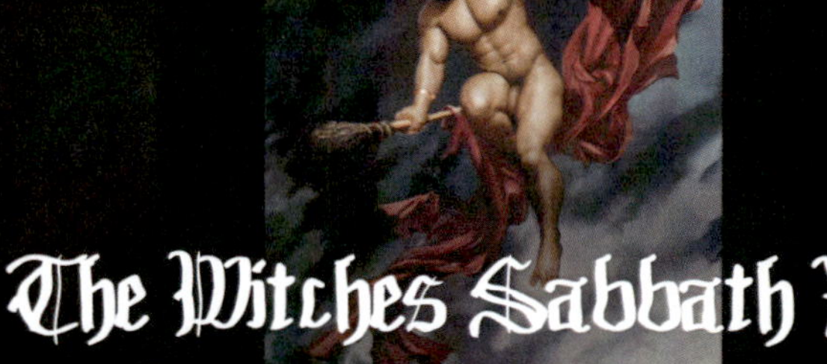

The Witches Sabbath V2

ASTRA ZERO SECOND REVAMP OF,
THE WITCHES SABBATH
BY LUIS RICARDO FALERO,
1880

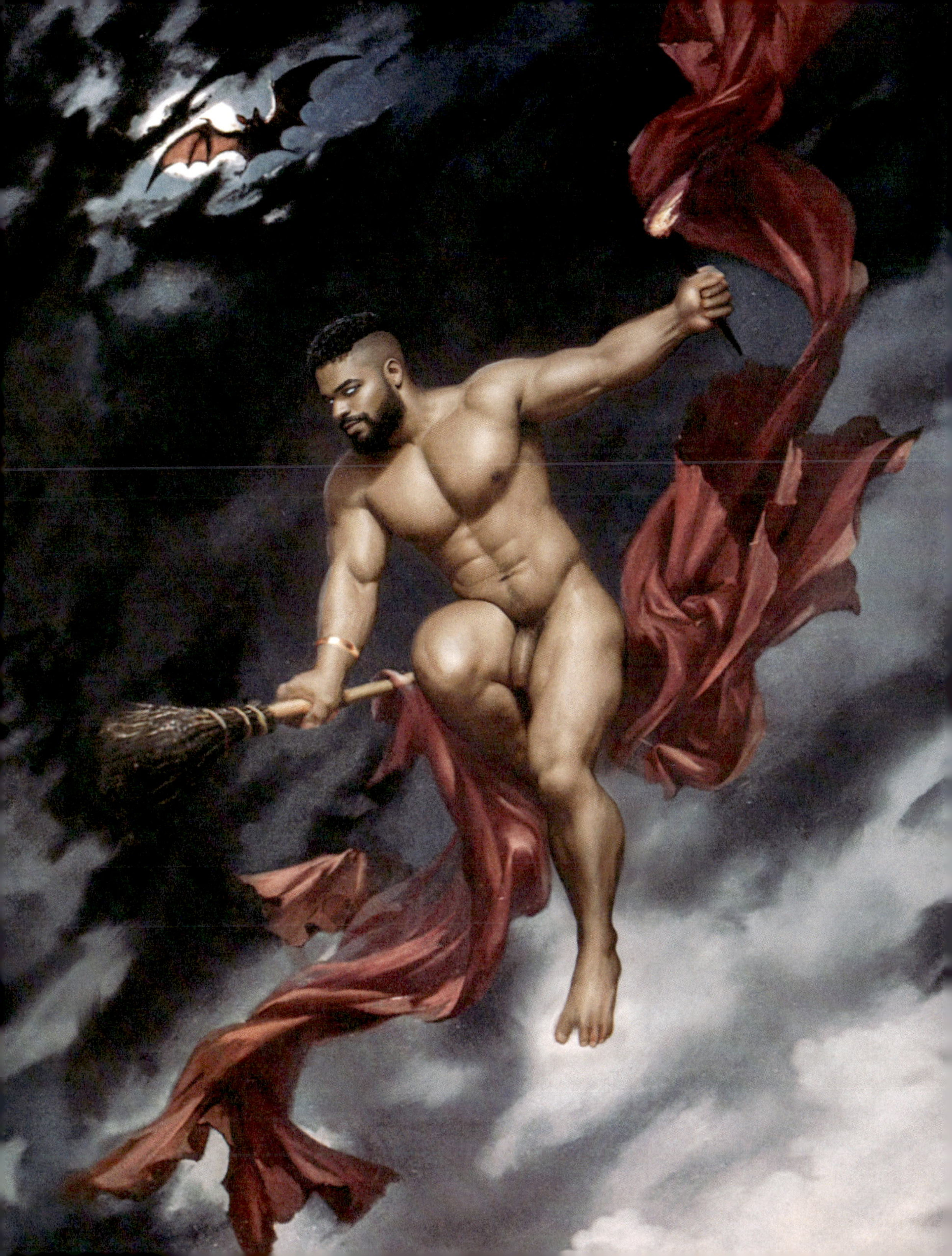

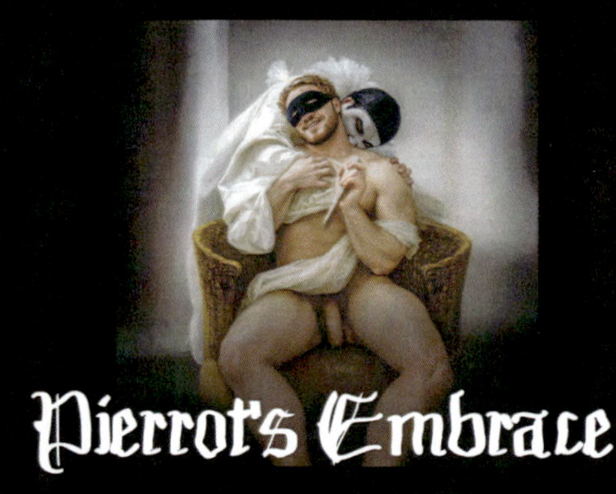

Pierrot's Embrace

ASTRA ZERO REVAMP OF,
PIERROT'S EMBRACE,
BY GUILLAUME SEIGNAC,
1900

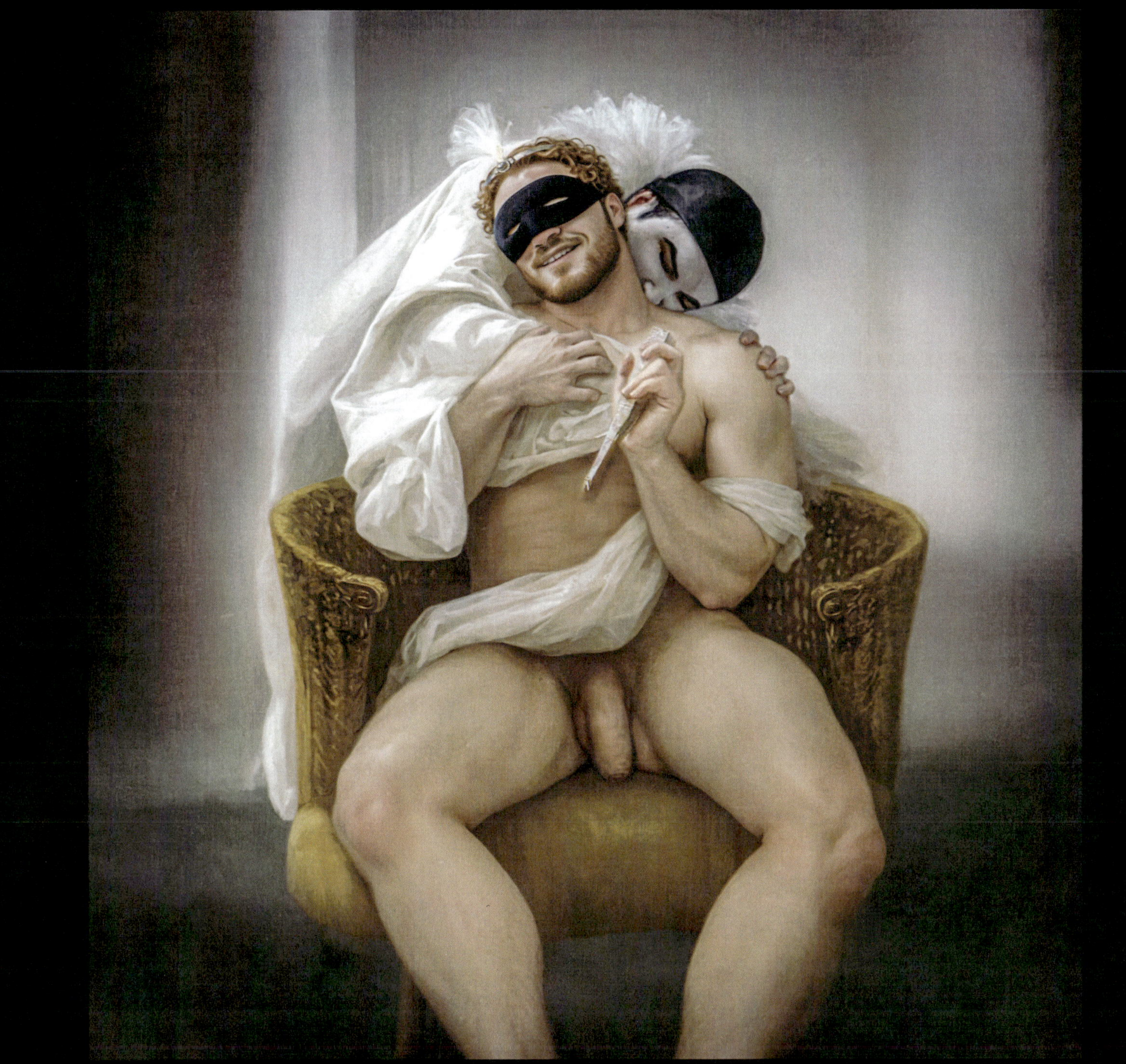

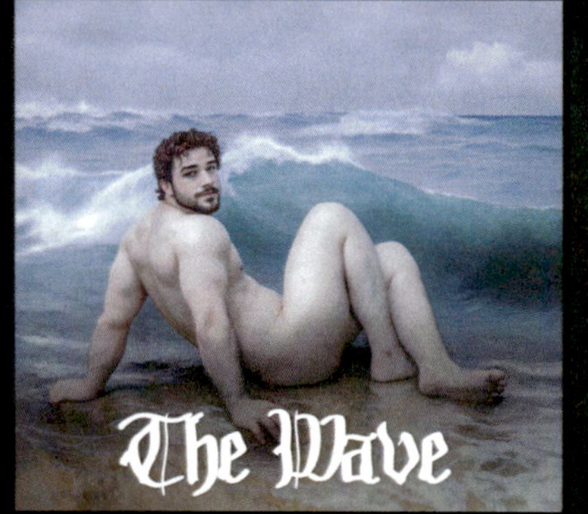

ASTRA ZERO REVAMP OF, THE WAVE,
BY WILLIAM-ADOLPHE BOUGUEREAU,
1896

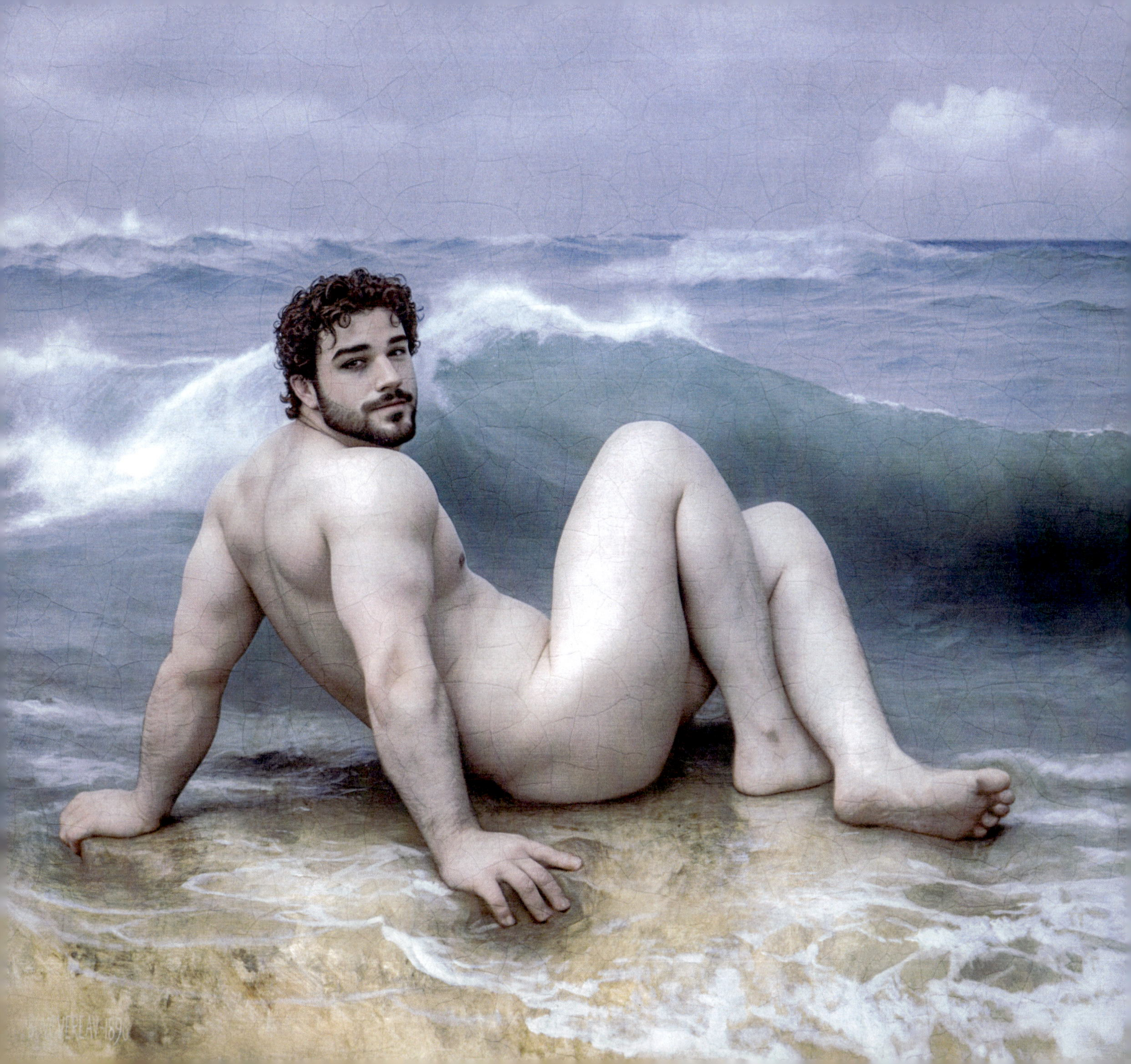
VERLAY 1890

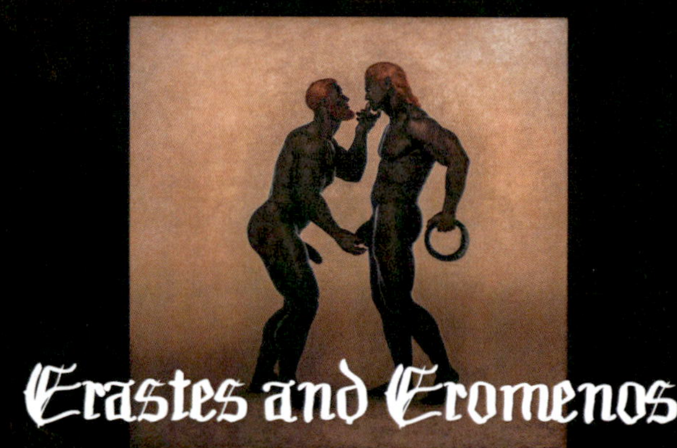

Erastes and Eromenos

ASTRA ZERO REVAMP OF,
ERASTES AND EROMENOS,
BY PAINTER OF CAMBRIDGE 47,
C.540 BCE

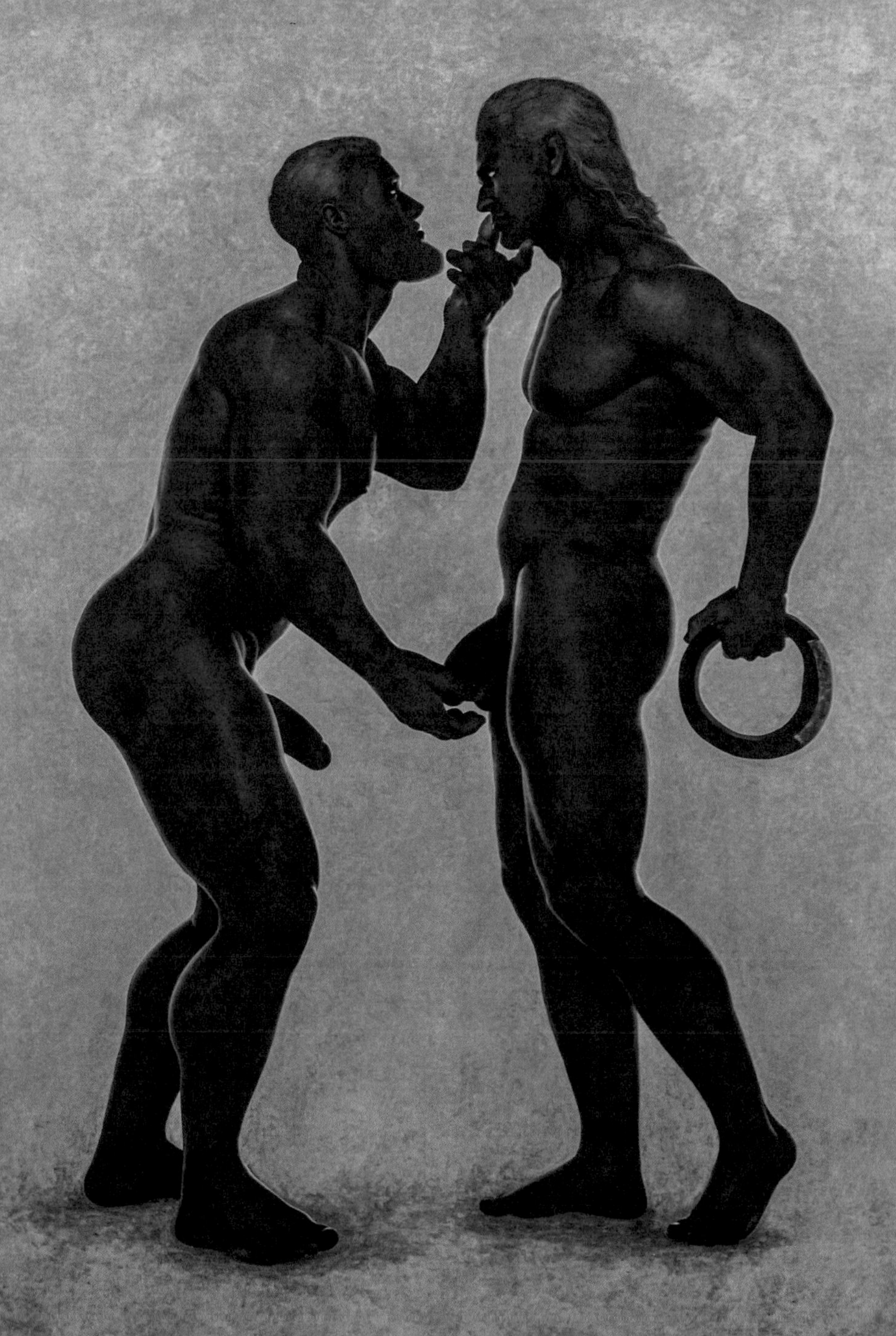

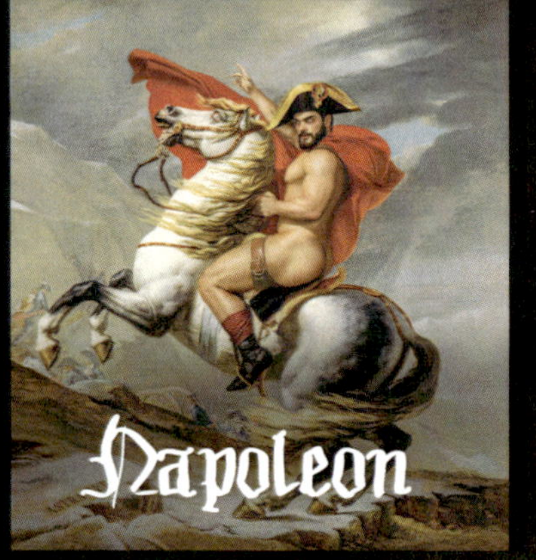

ASTRA ZERO REVAMP OF,
NAPOLEON CROSSING THE ALPS,
BY JACQUES-LOUIS DAVID, 1802

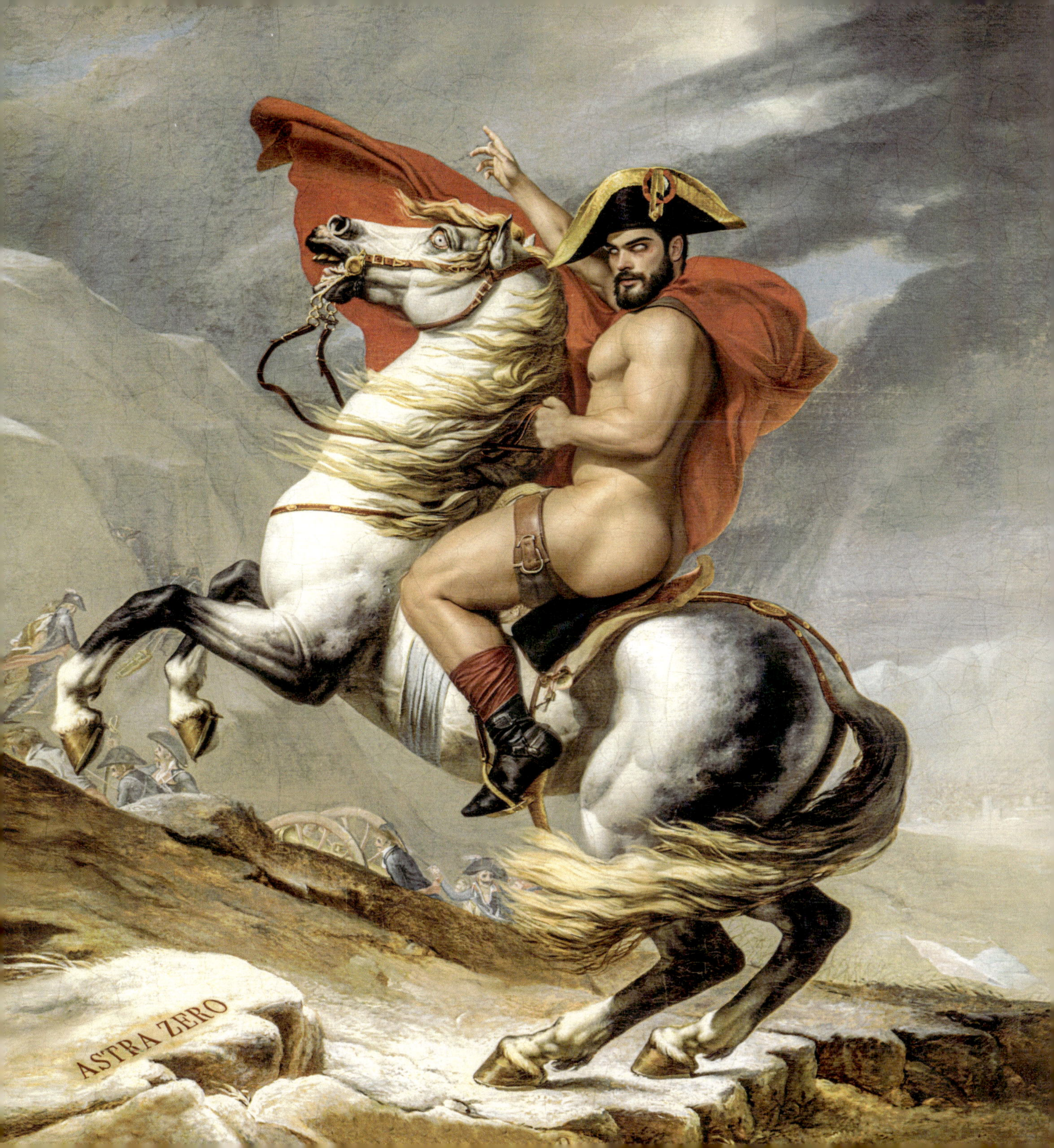
ASTRA ZERO

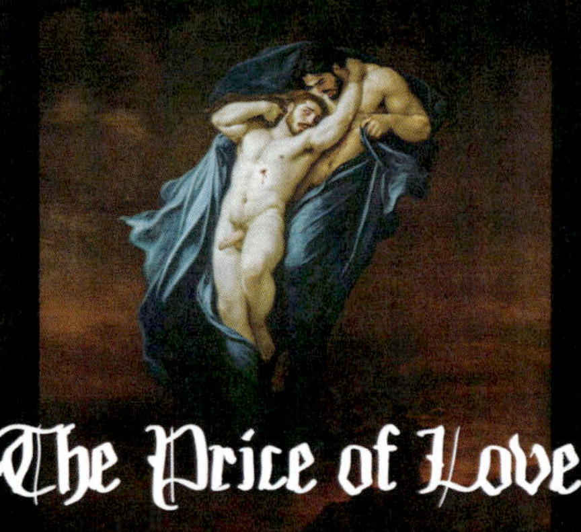

The Price of Love

ASTRA ZERO REVAMP OF,
PAOLO AND FRANCESCA DA RIMINI,
BY GUSTAVE DORE, 1863

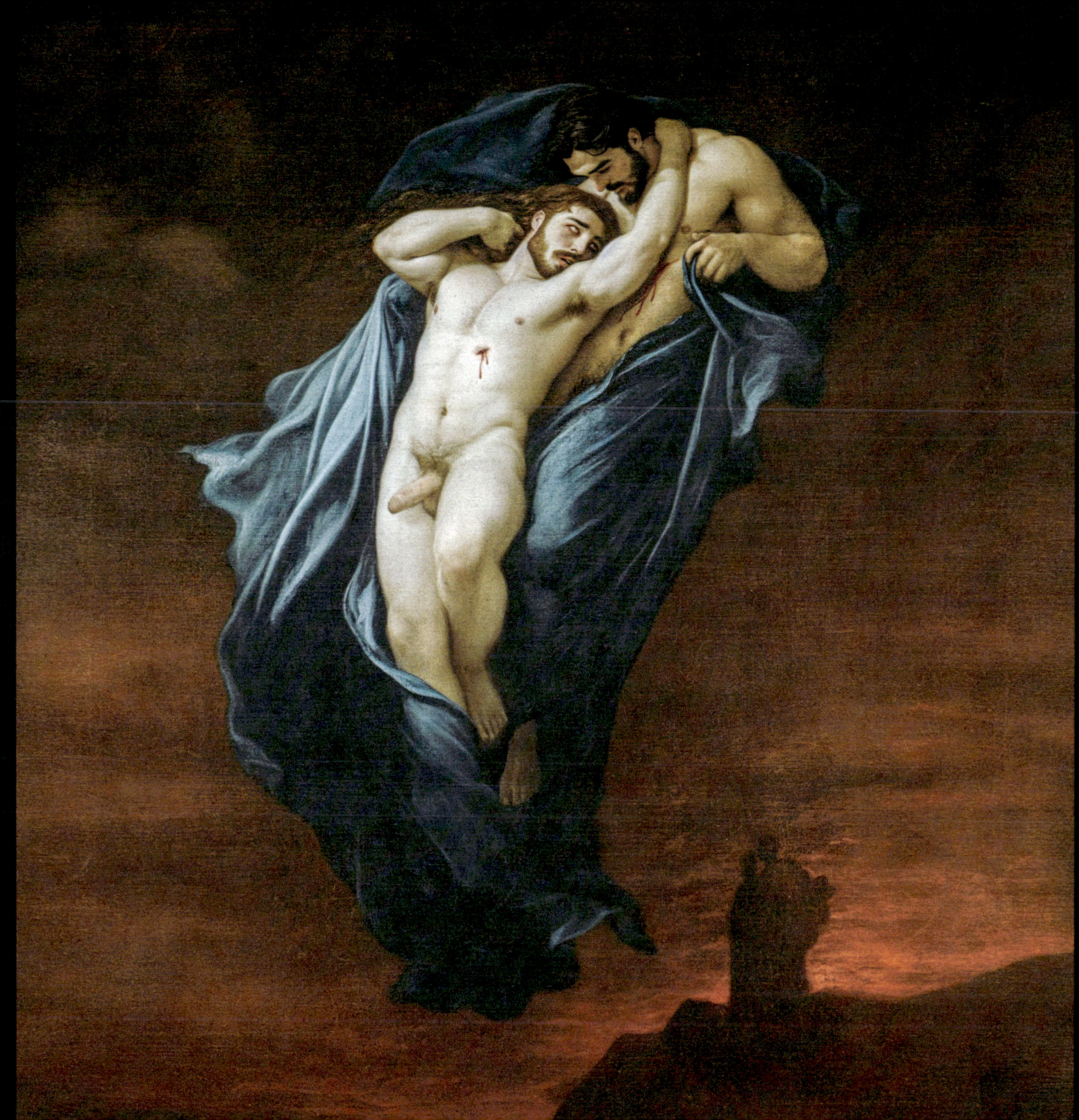

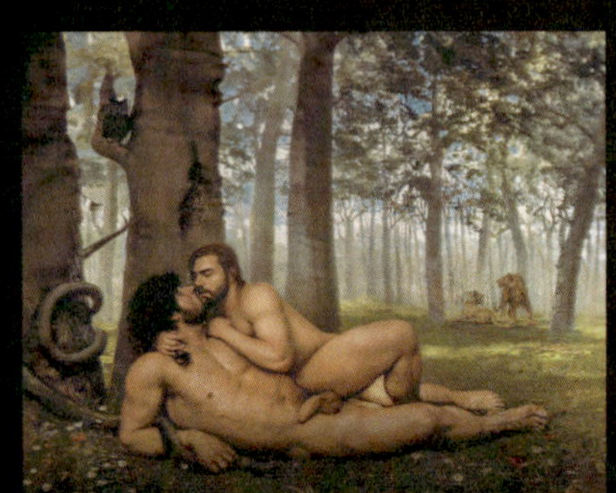

The First kiss of Adam & Steve

ASTRA ZERO REVAMP OF,
THE FIRST KISS OF ADAM AND EVE,
BY SALVADOR VINIEGRA, 1891

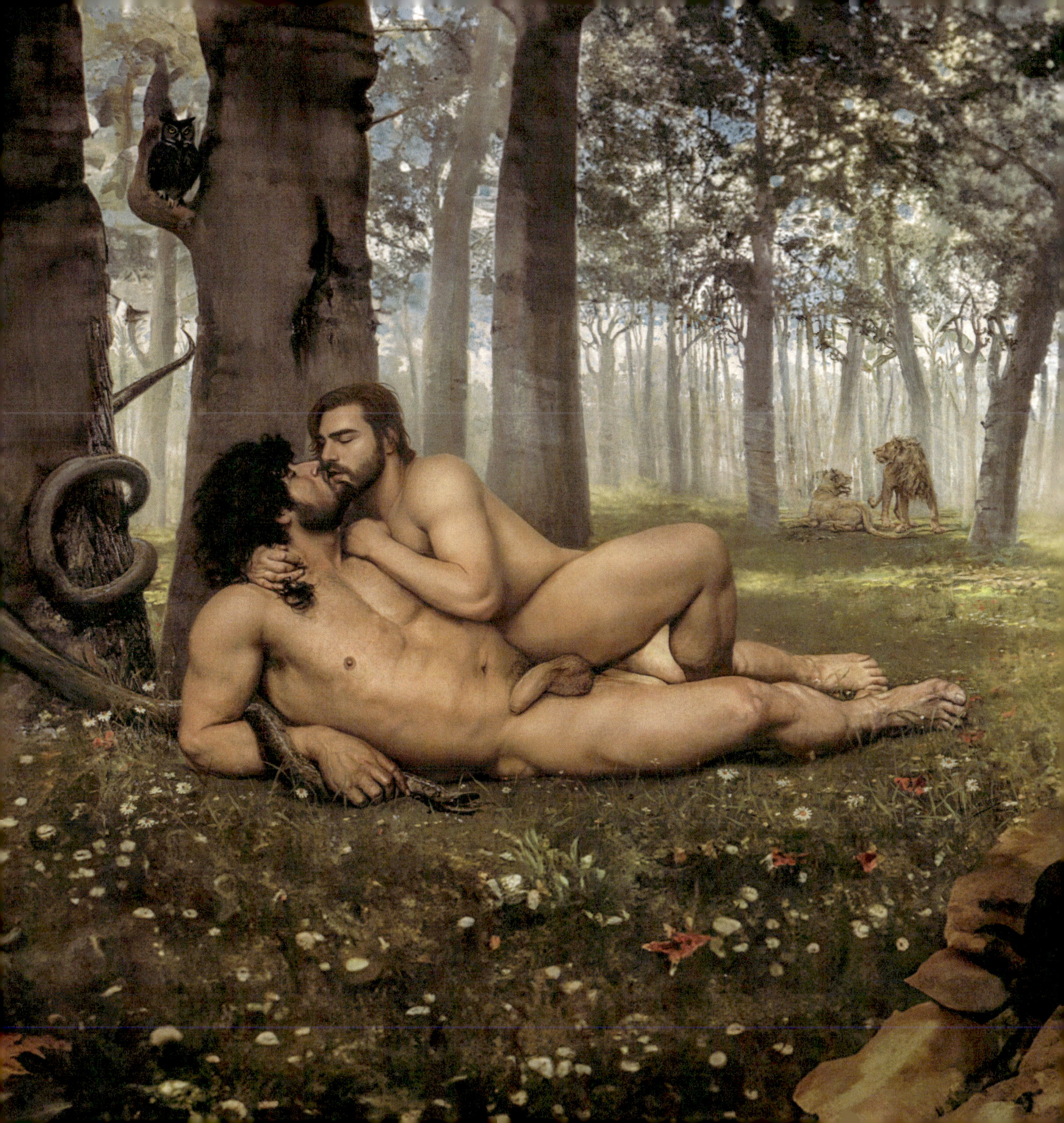

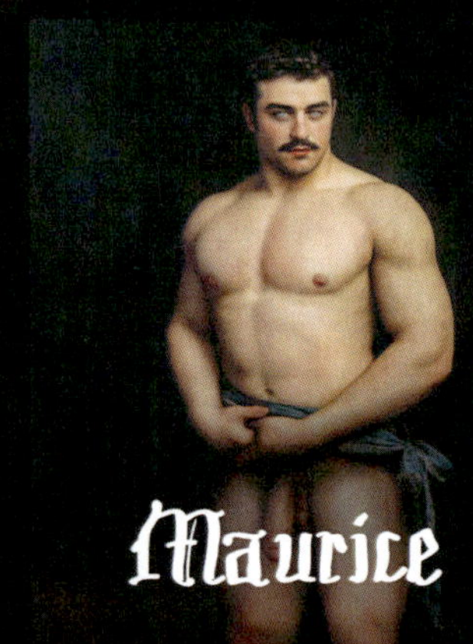

ASTRA ZERO REVAMP OF,
PORTRAIT DE MAURICE DERIAZ,
BY GUSTAVE COURTOIS,
1907

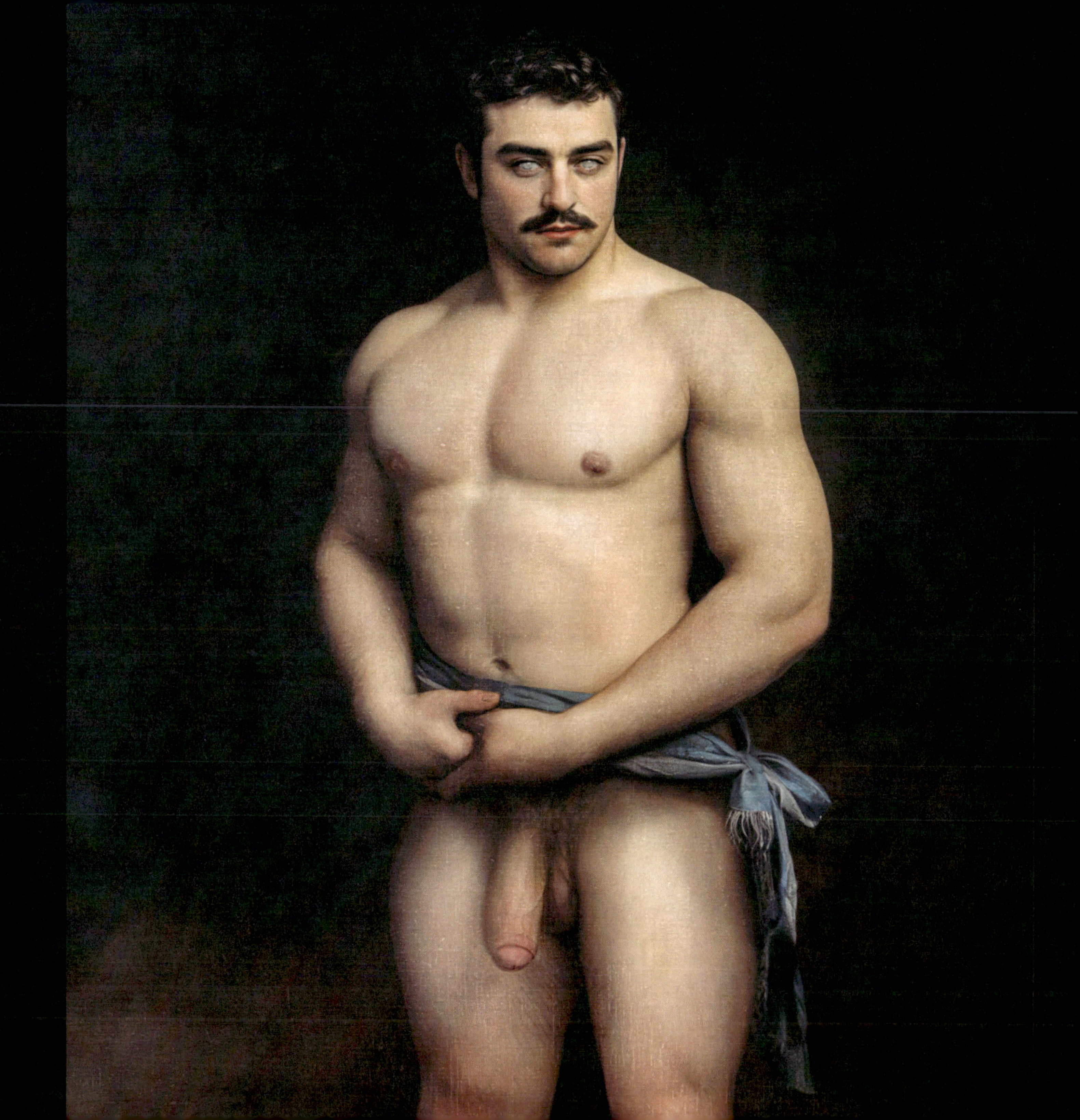

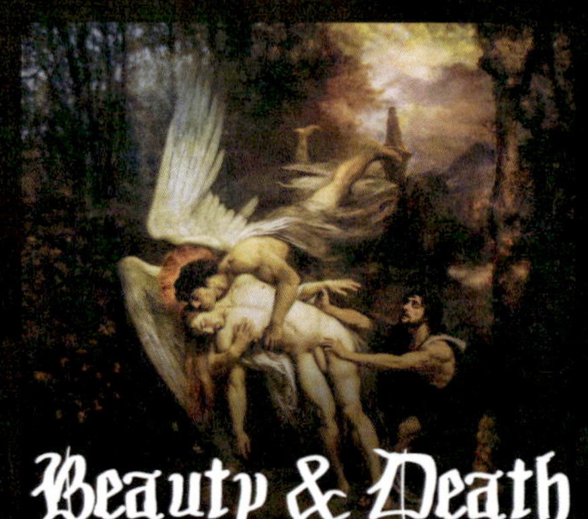

ASTRA ZERO REVAMP OF,
LA JEUNE FILLE ET LA MORT,
BY HENRY LEVY, 1900

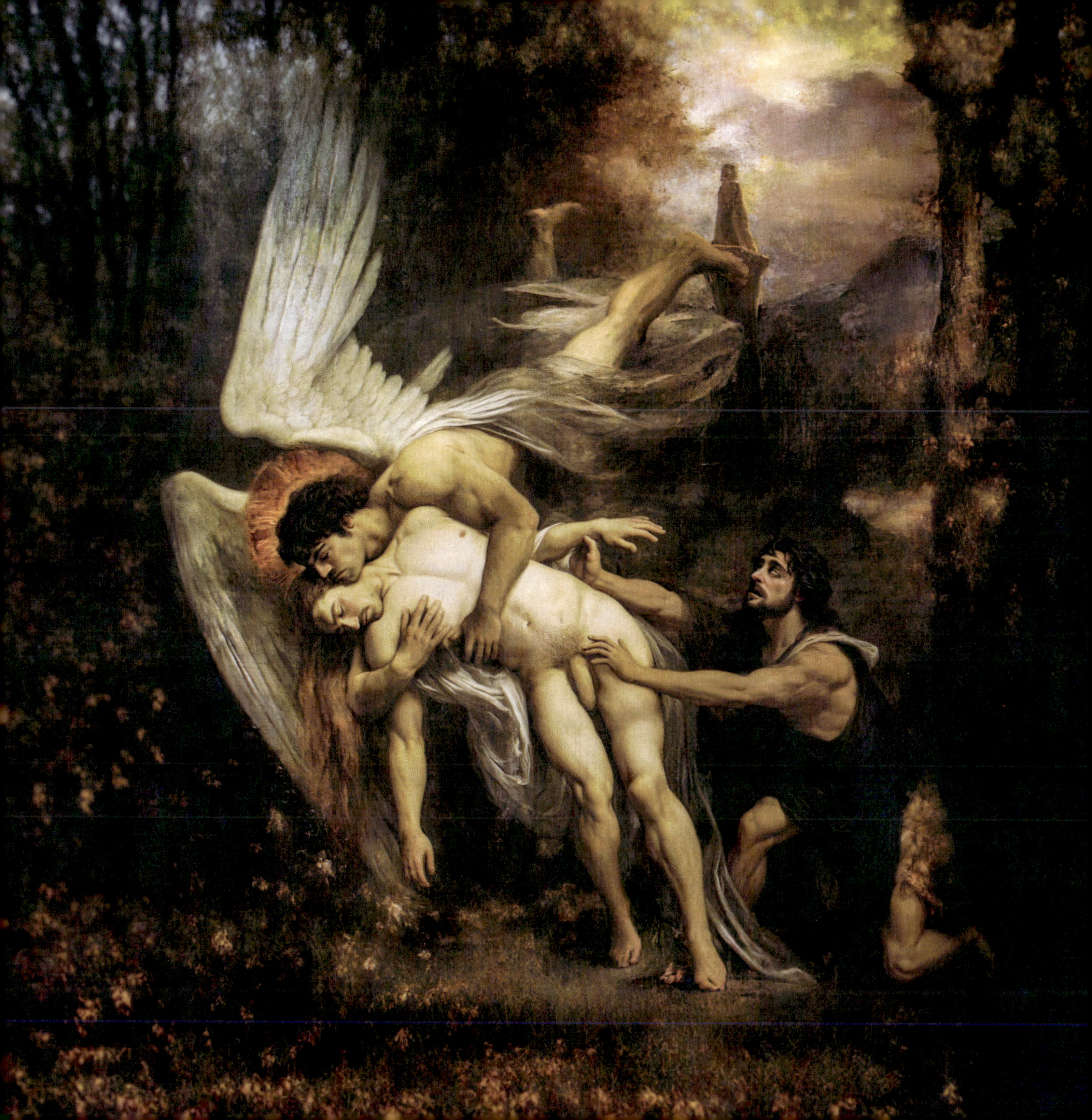

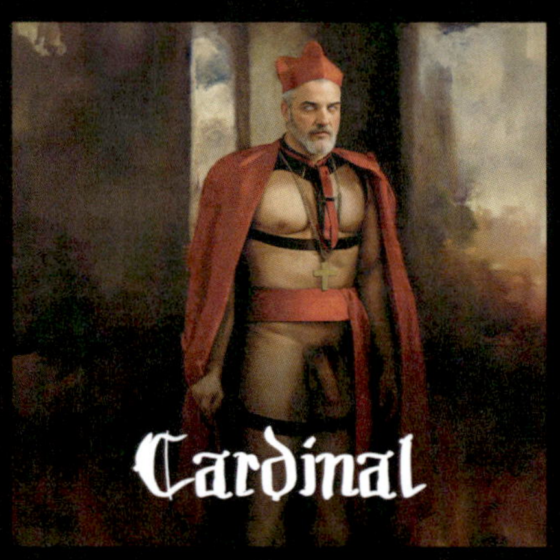

ASTRA ZERO GOTHIC REVAMP OF,
CARDINAL MERCIER,
BY CECILIA BEAUX,
1919

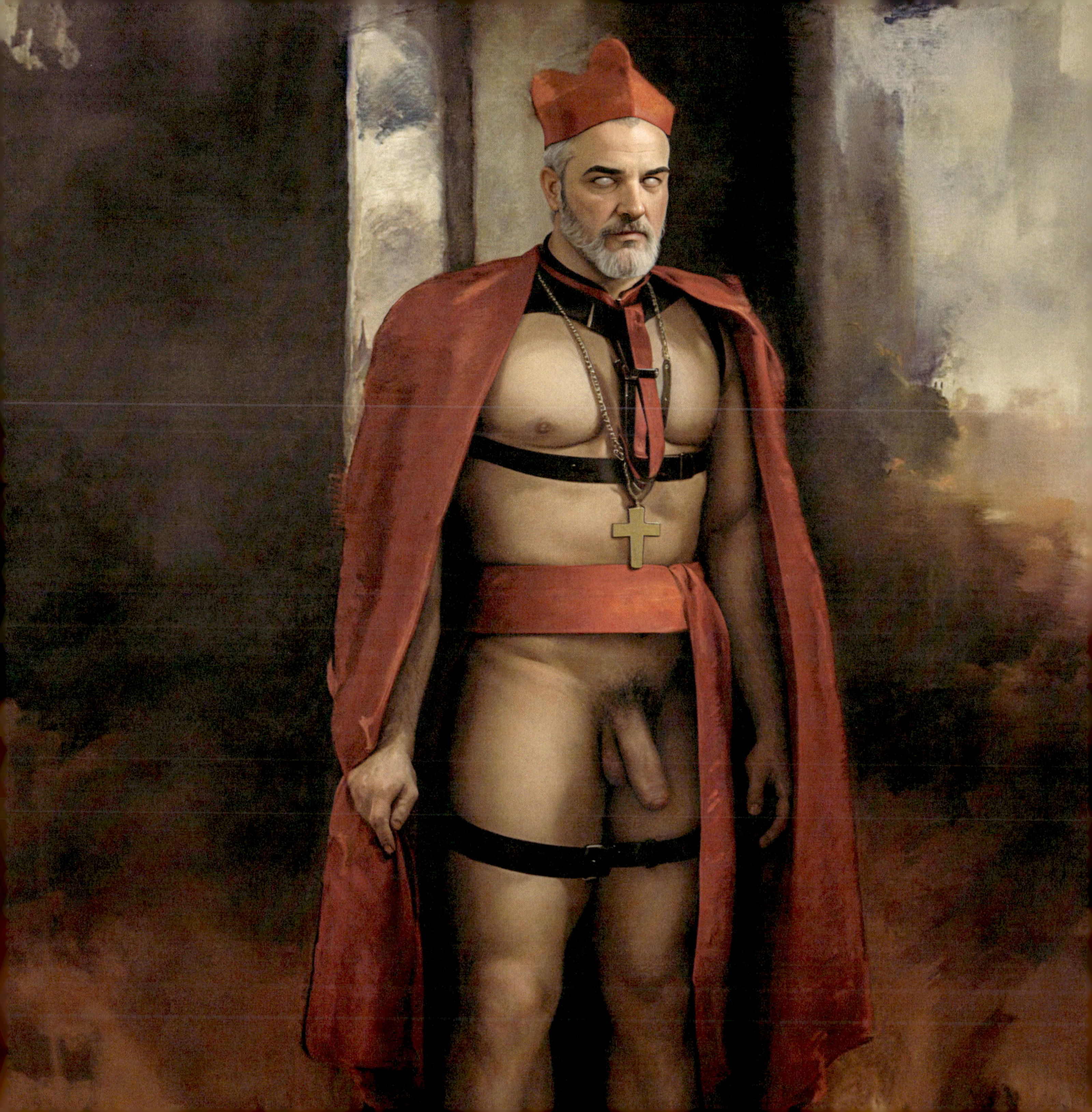

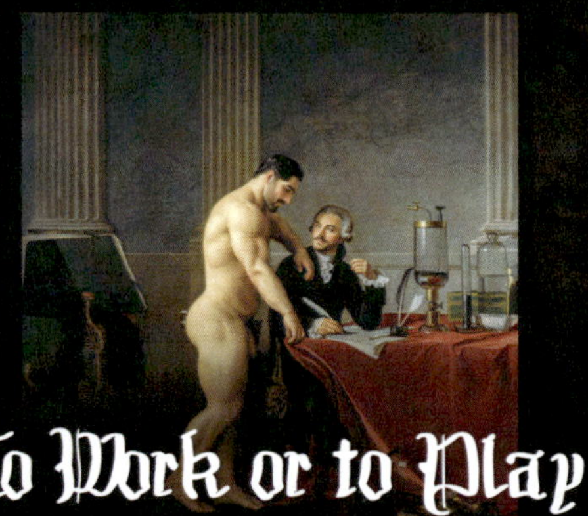

To Work or to Play

ASTRA ZERO REVAMP OF, PORTRAIT DE
MONSIEUR DE LAVOISIER ET SA FEMME
MARIE-ANNE PIERRETTE PAULZE,
BY JACQUES-LOUIS DAVID, 1788

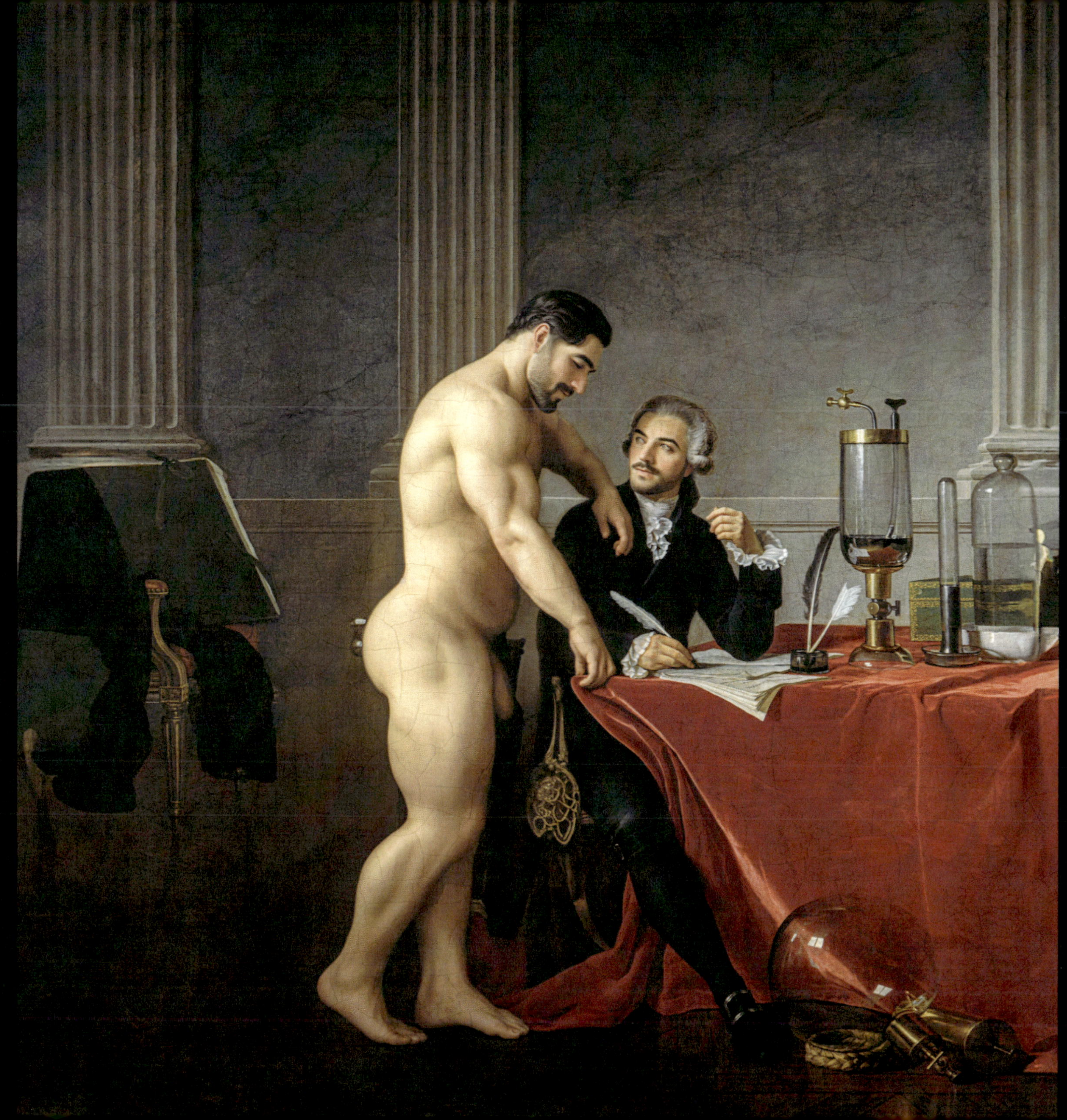

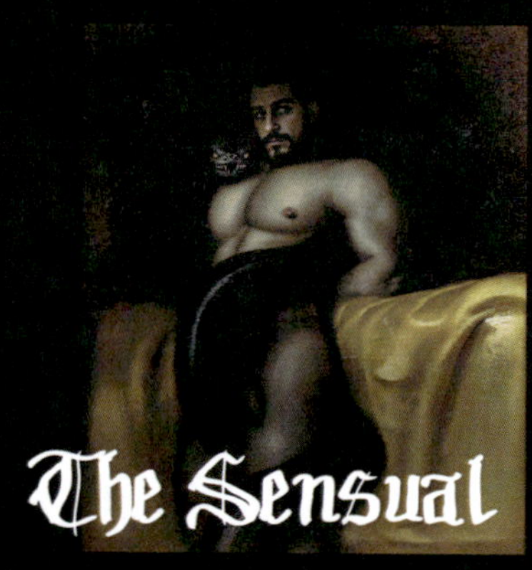

ASTRA ZERO REVAMP OF,
THE SENSUAL, BY FRANZ STUCK,
1891

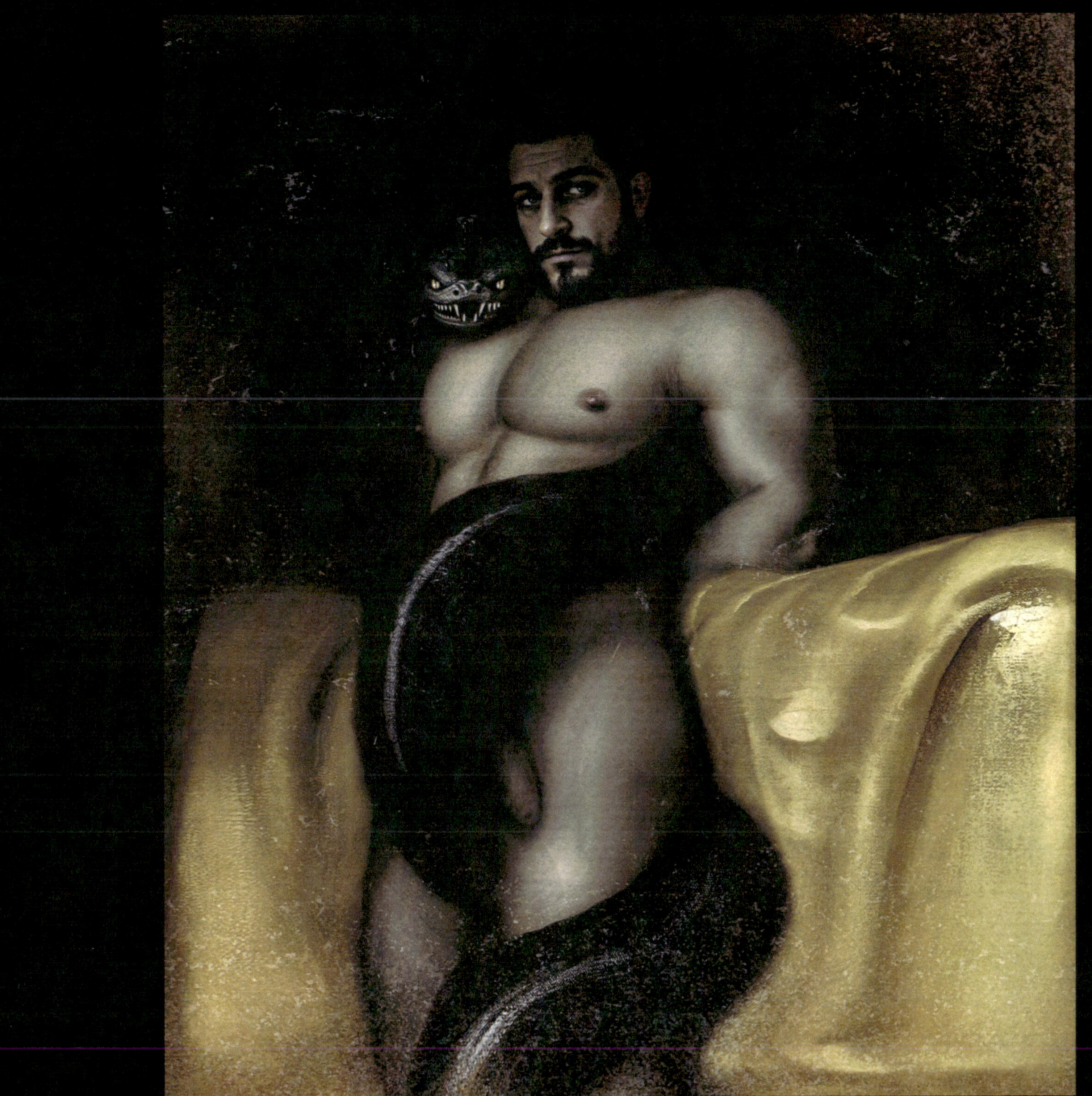

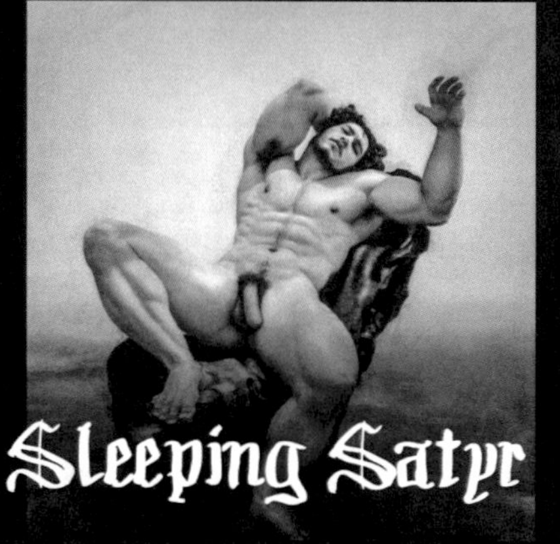

ASTRA ZERO REVAMP OF THE SCULPTURE,
SLEEPING SATYR / BARBERINI FAUN,
BY UNKNOWN ARTIST
(RESTORED BY GIUSEPPE GIORGETTI),
CIRCA 220 BCE

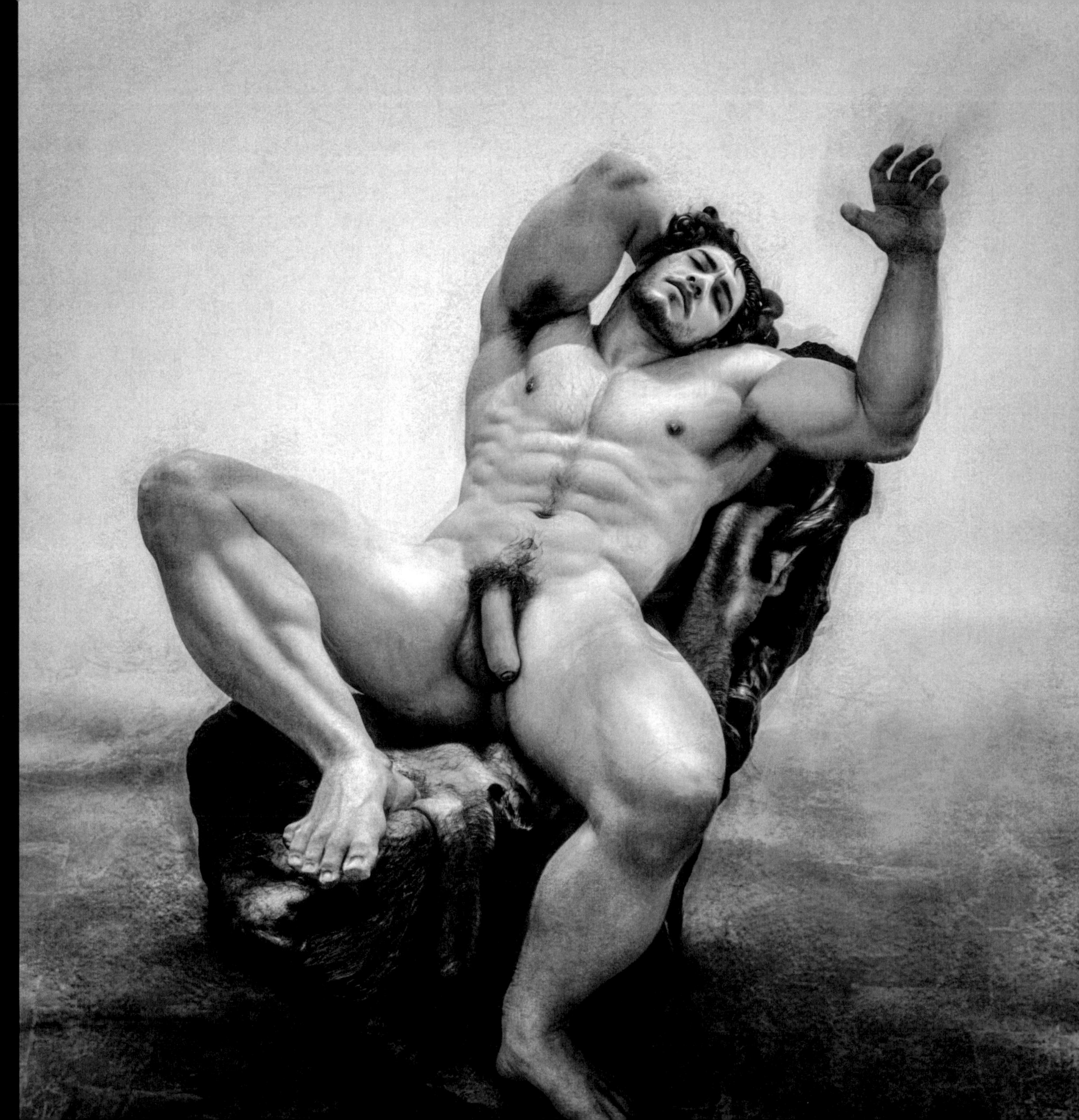

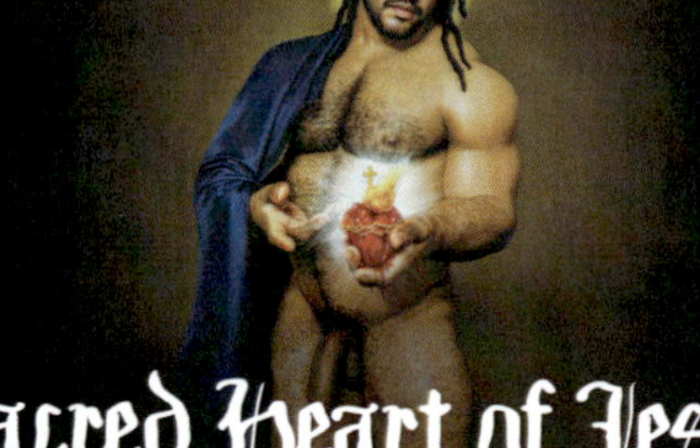

Sacred Heart of Jesus

ASTRA ZERO REVAMP OF,
SACRED HEART OF JESUS,
BY POMPEO BATONI,
1767

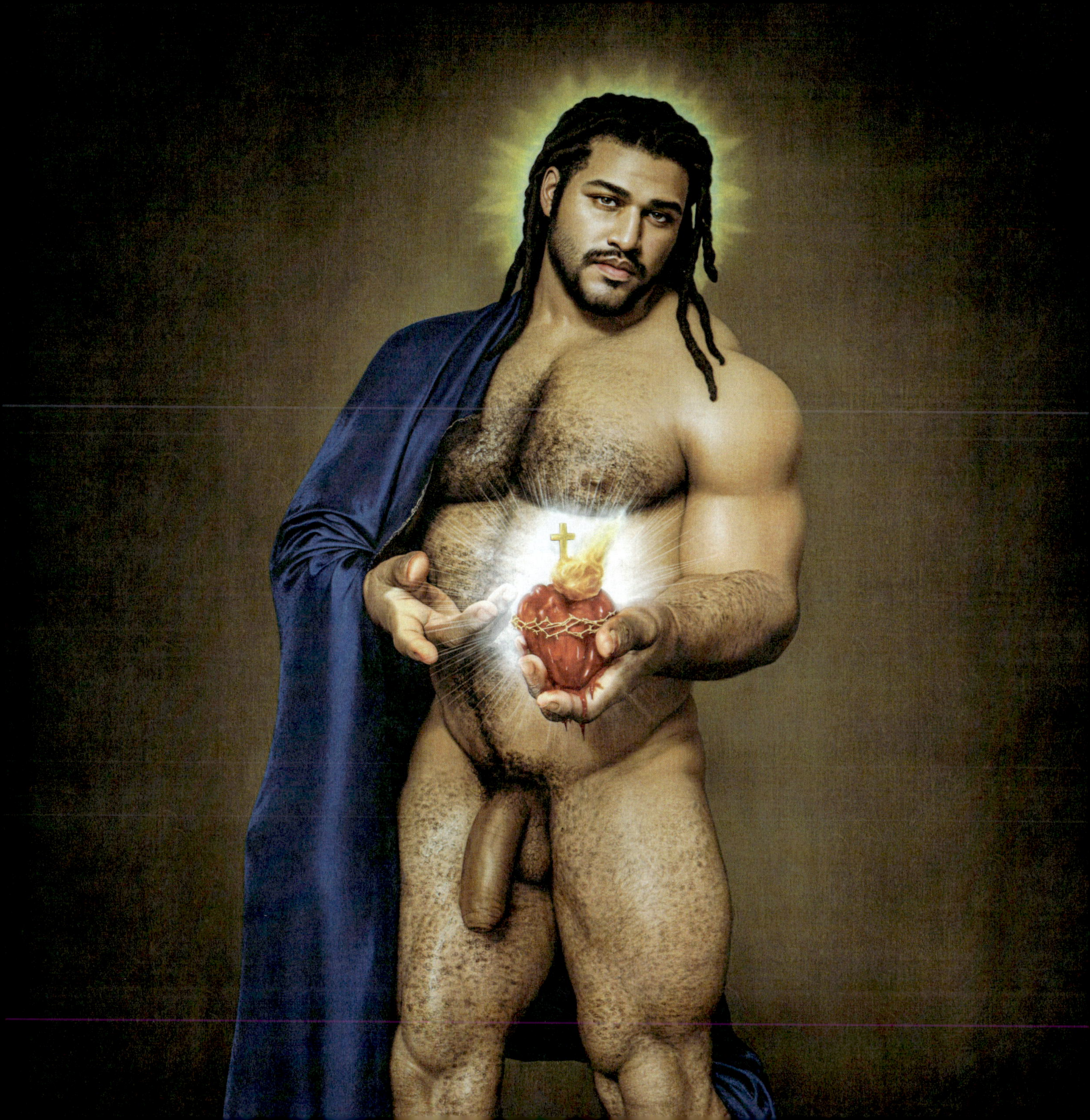

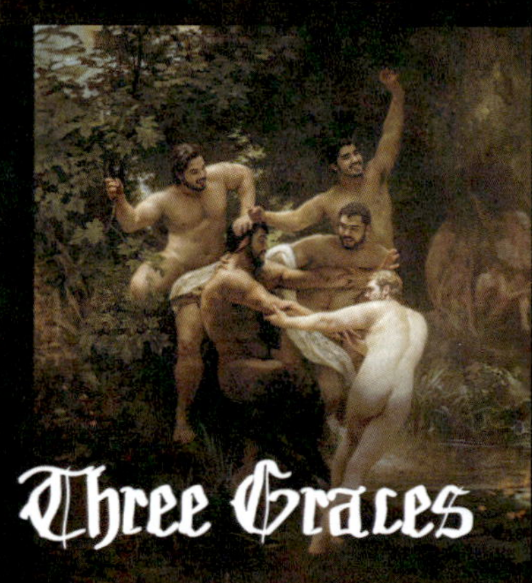

ASTRA ZERO REVAMP OF,
DRIE GRATIEN,
BY PETER PAUL RUBENS,
1630

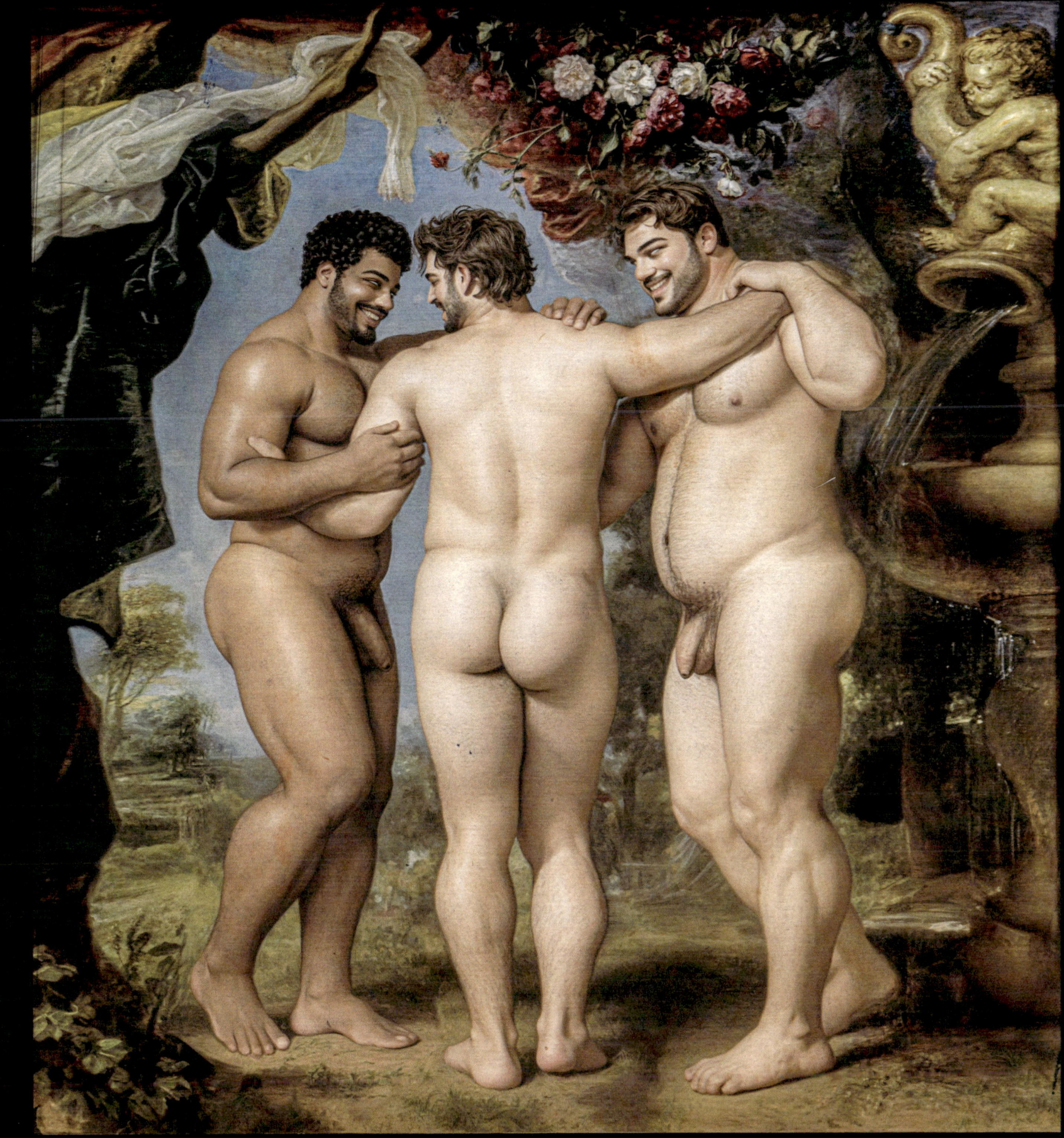

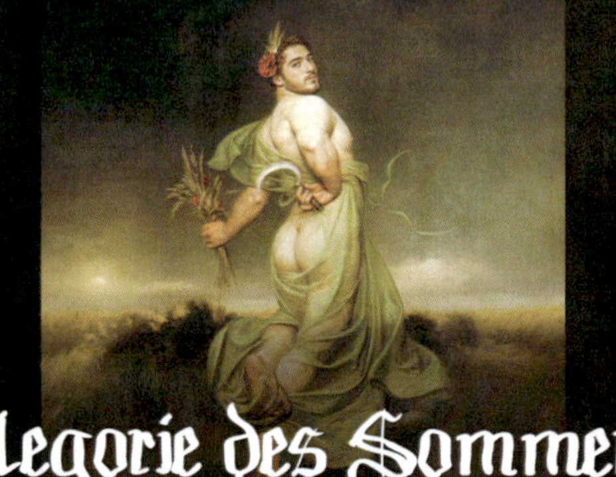

Allegorie des Sommers

ASTRA ZERO REVAMP OF,
ALLEGORIE DES SOMMERS,
BY FRANTISEK BOHUMIL DOUBEK,
1905

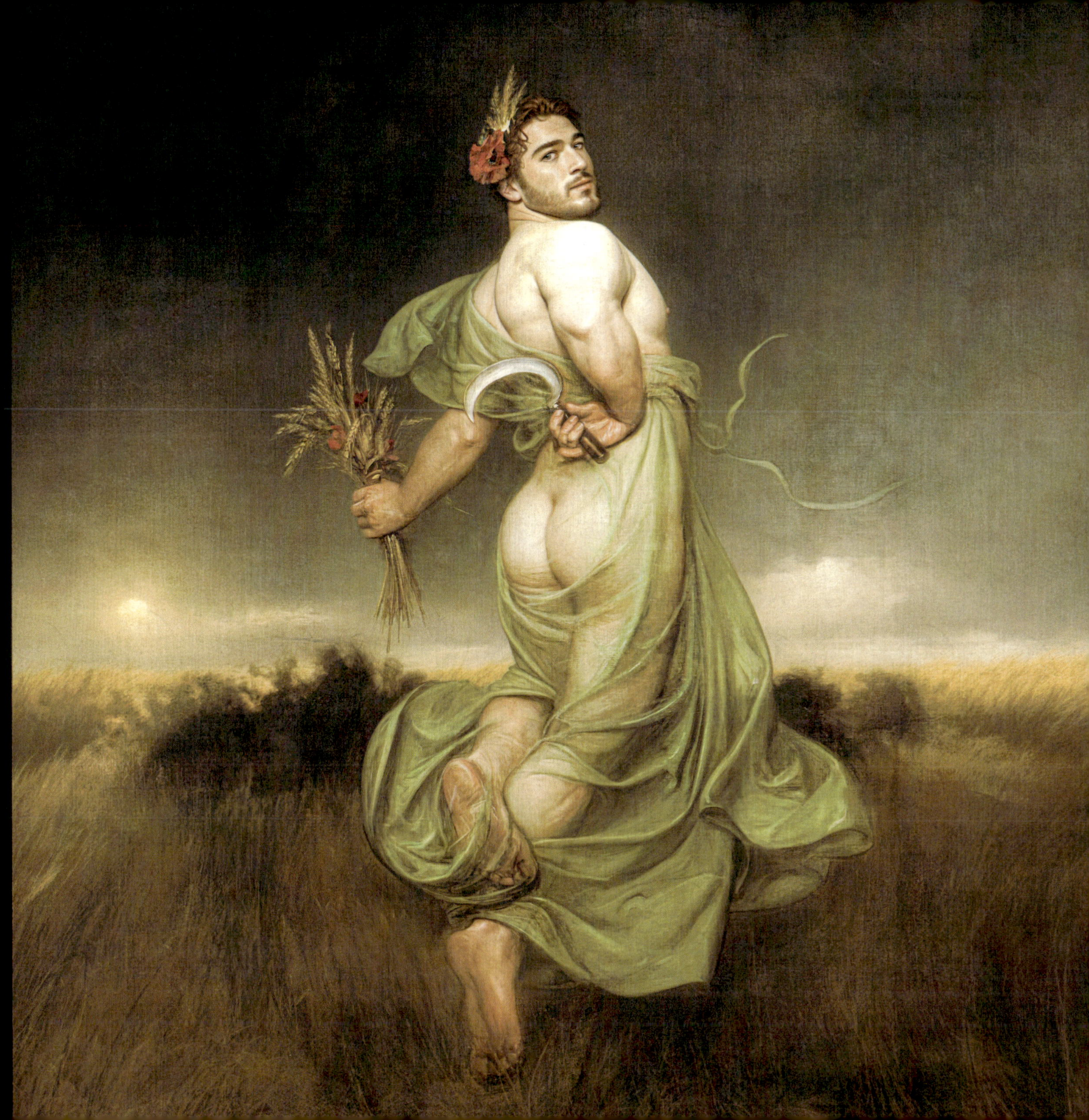

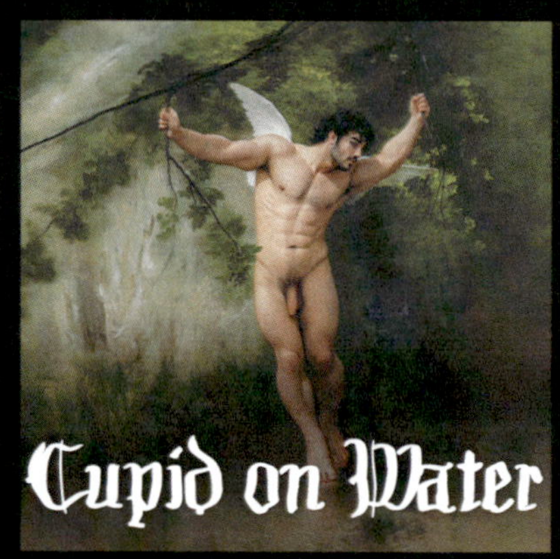

ASTRA ZERO REVAMP OF,
AMOUR VOLTIGEANT SUR LES EAUX,
BY WILLIAM-ADOLPHE BOUGUEREAU,
1900

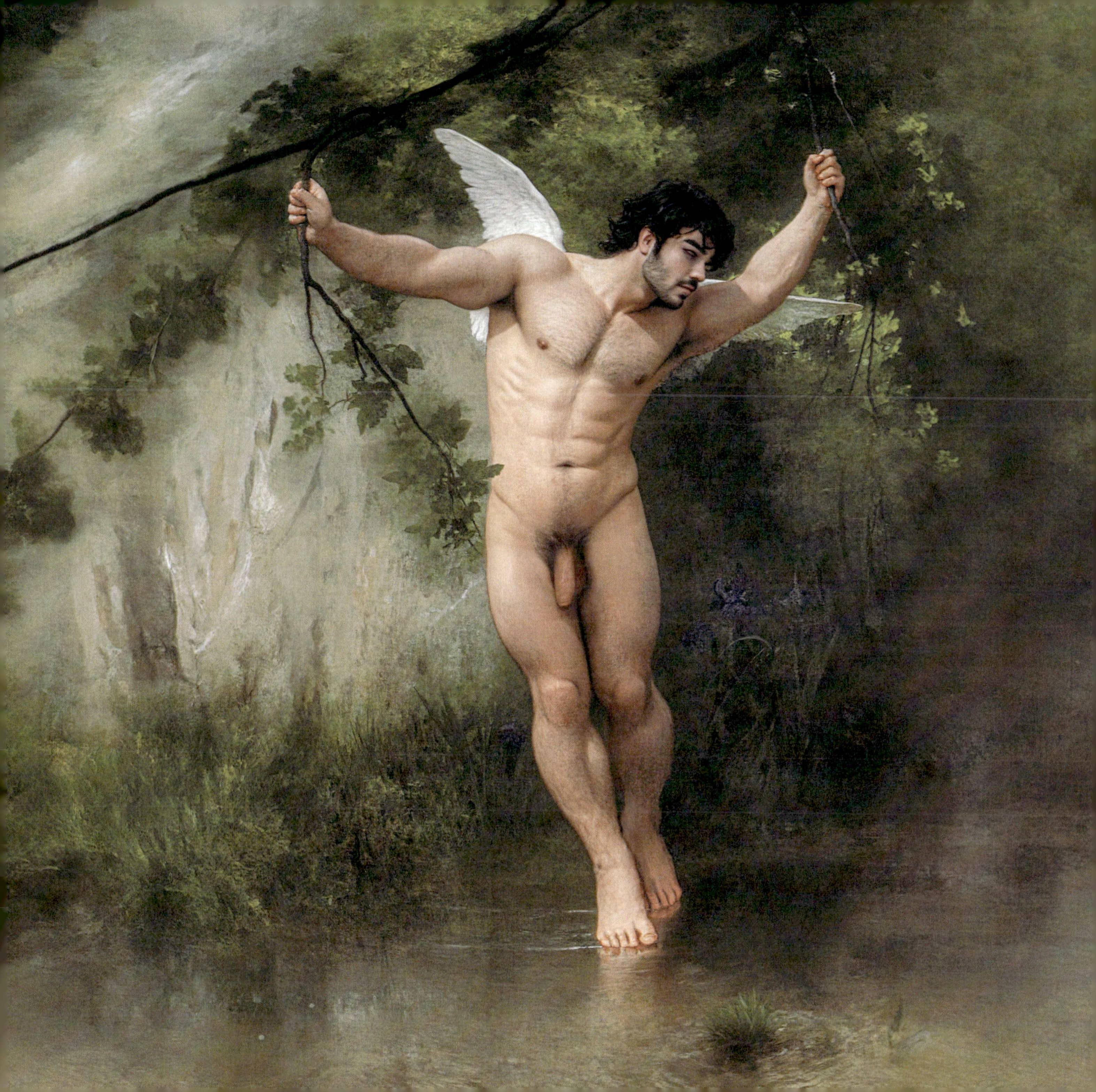

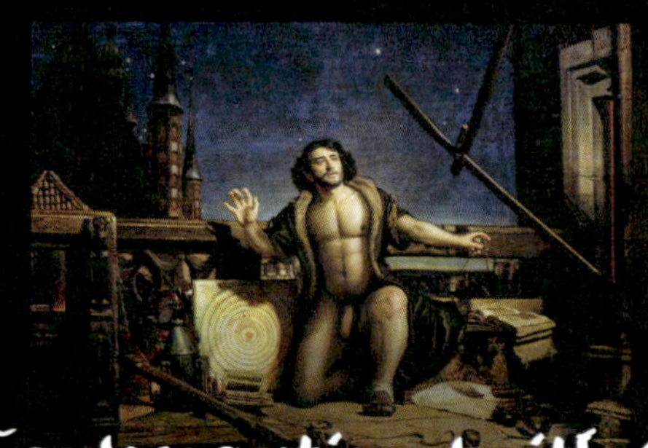

A Conversation with God.

ASTRA ZERO REVAMP OF,
ASTRONOM KOPERNIK,
CZYLI ROZMOWA Z BOGIEM,
BY JAN MATEJKO, 1873

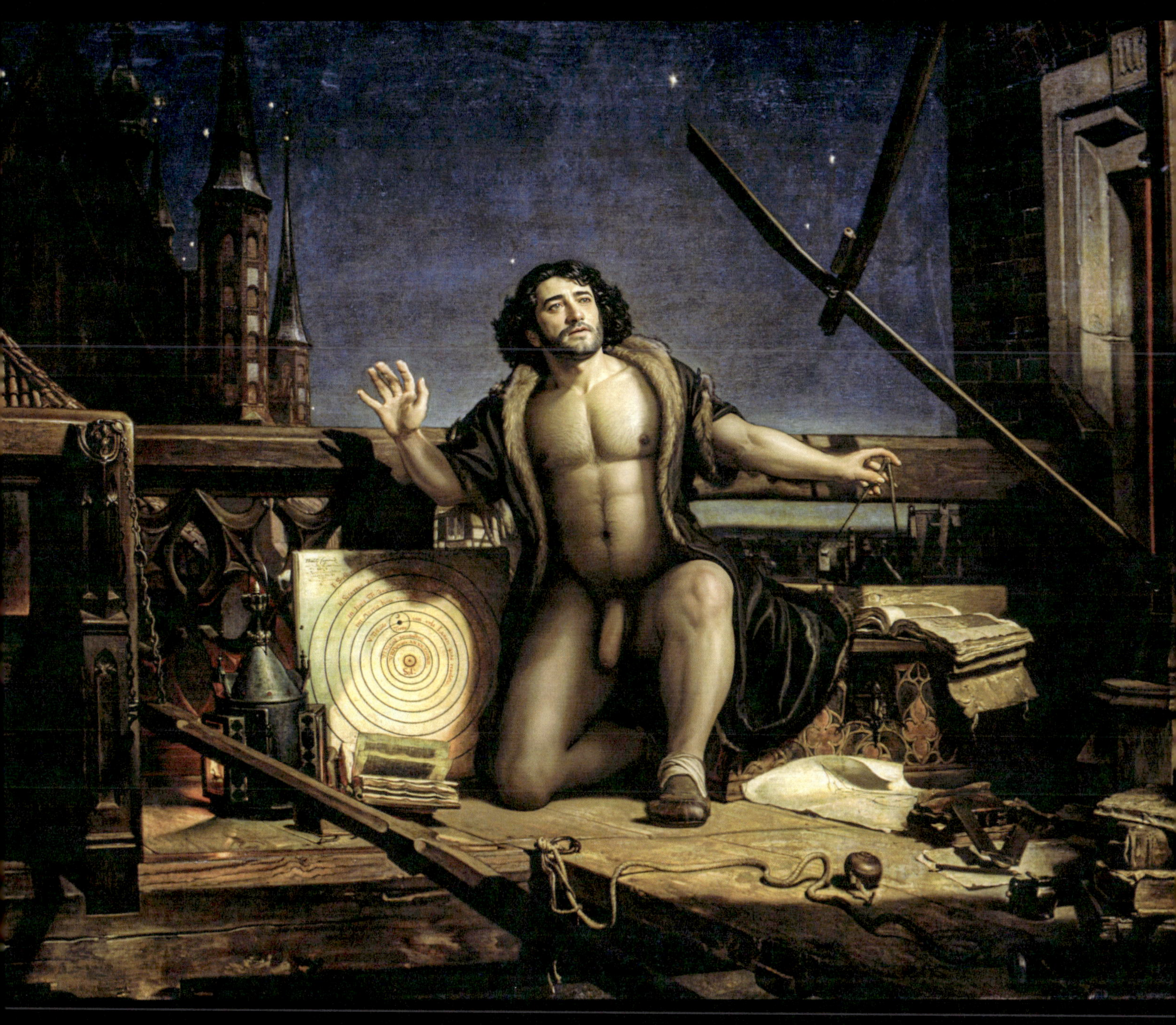

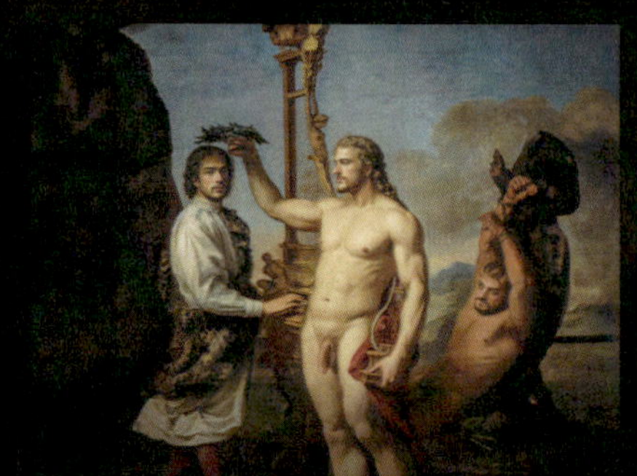

Crowned by Apollo

ASTRA ZERO REVAMP OF,
MARCANTONIO PASQUILINI CROWNED BY
APOLLO, BY ANDREA SACCHI,
1641

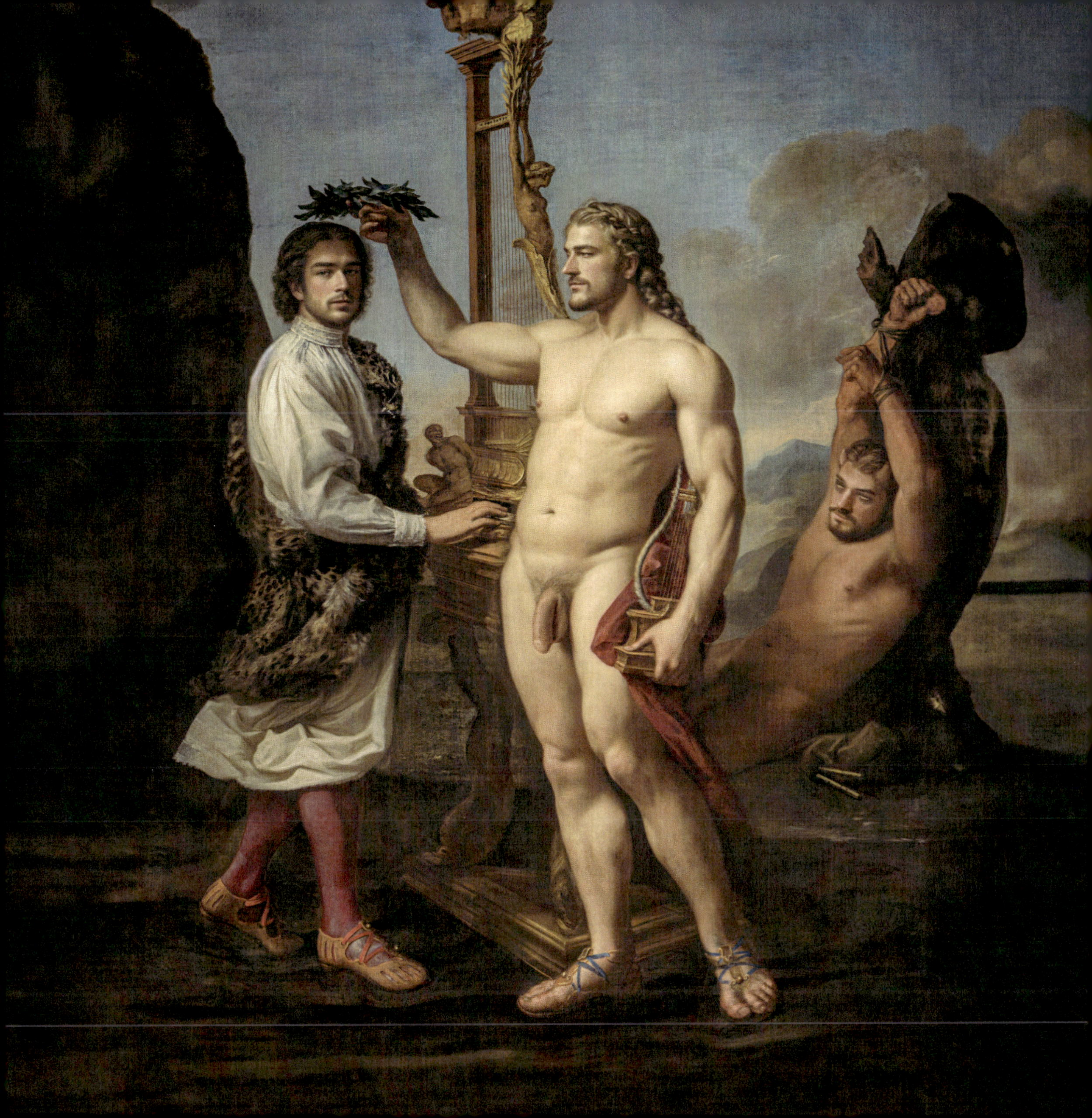

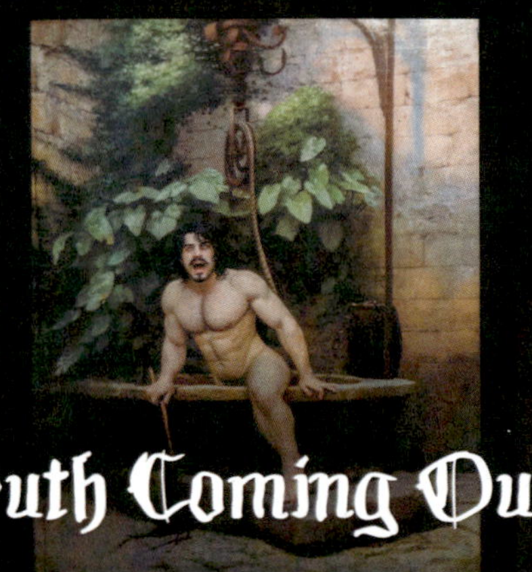

Truth Coming Out

ASTRA ZERO REVAMP OF,
TRUTH COMING OUT OF HER WELL,
BY JEAN-LEON GEROME, 1896

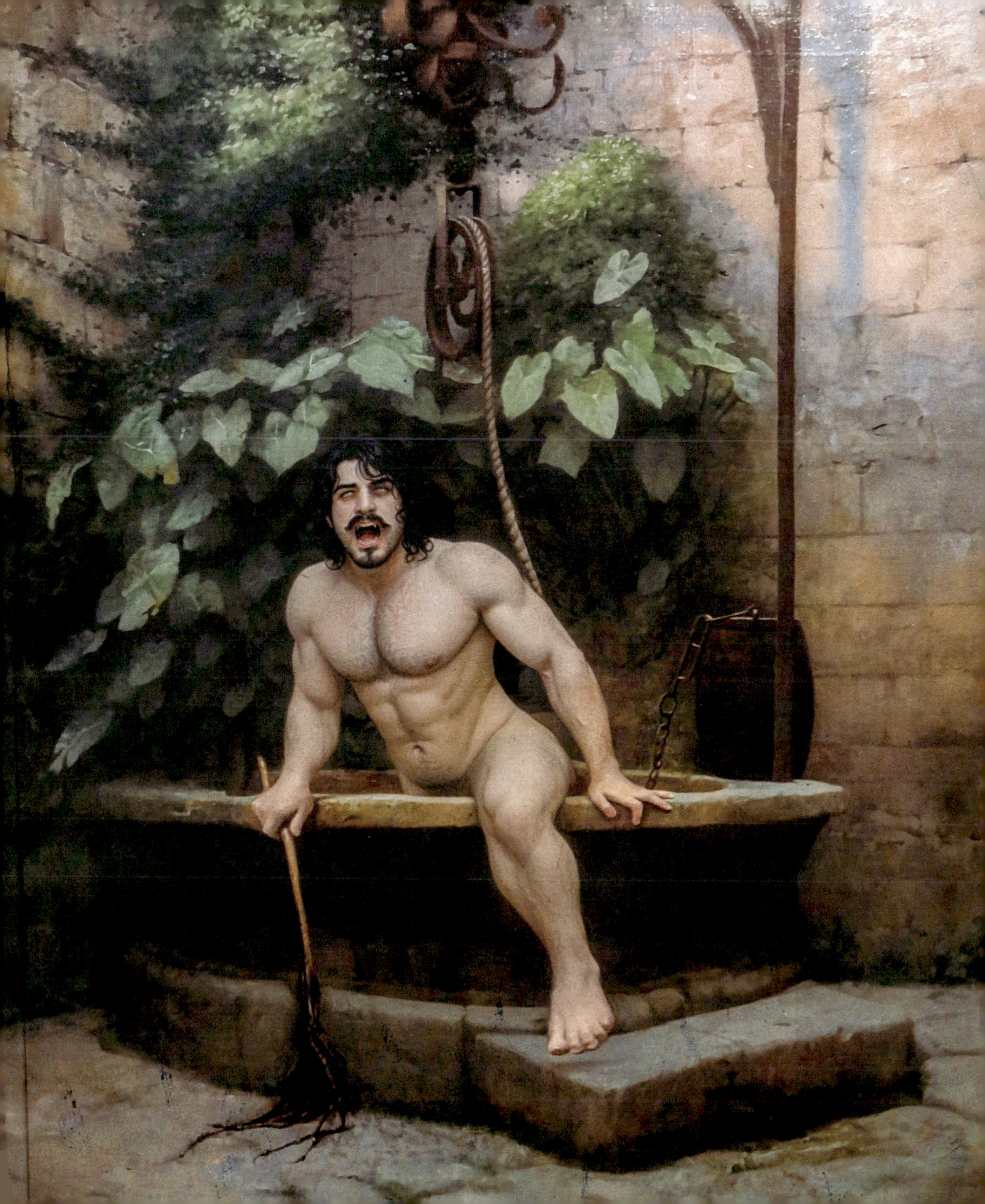

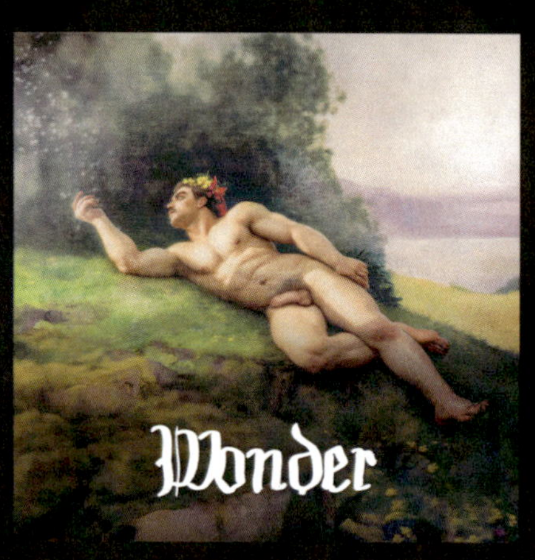

ASTRA ZERO REVAMP OF,
A STUDY OF MAURICE DERIAZ,
BY GUSTAVE COURTOIS,
ESTIMATED EARLY 1900S

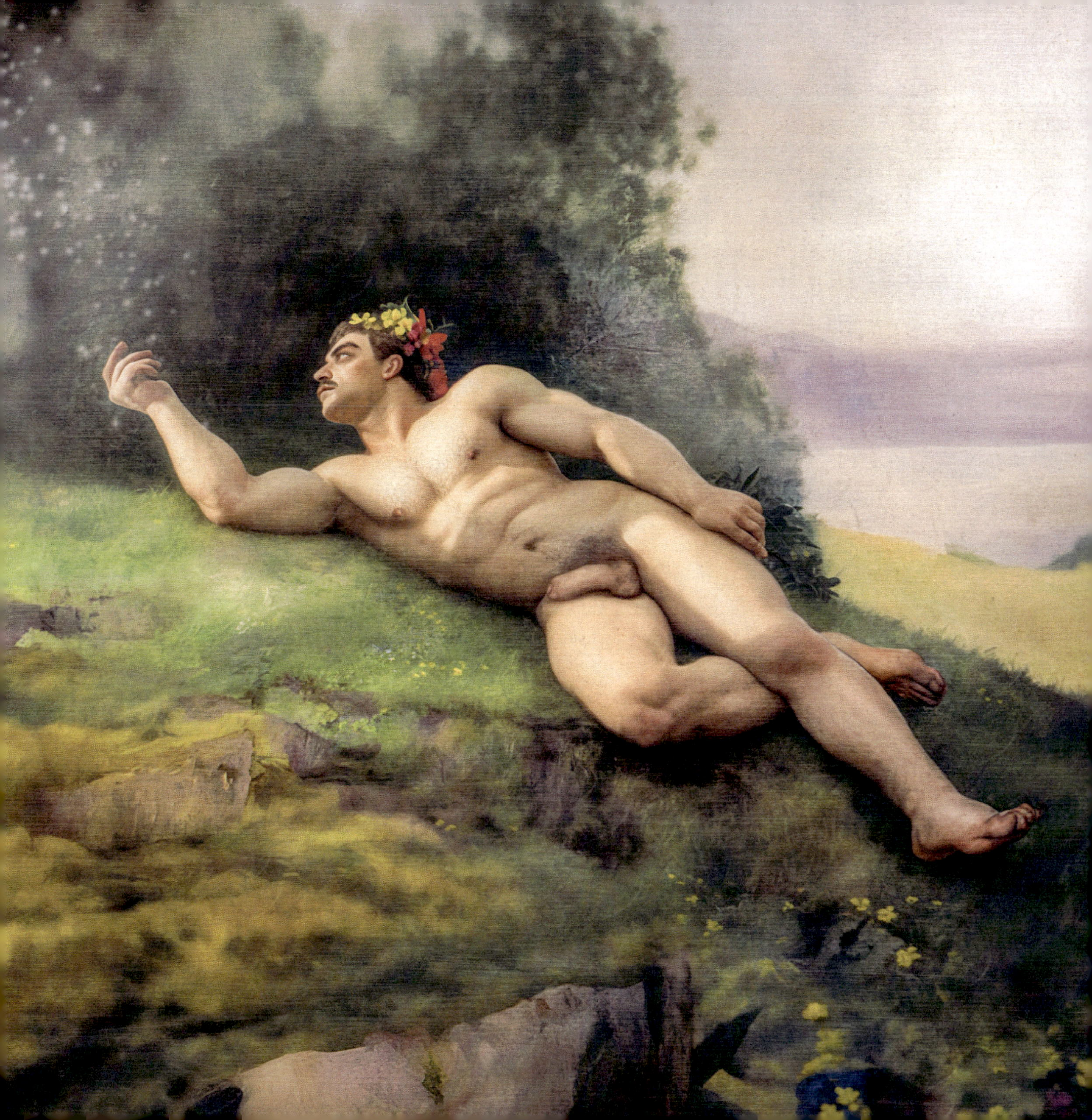

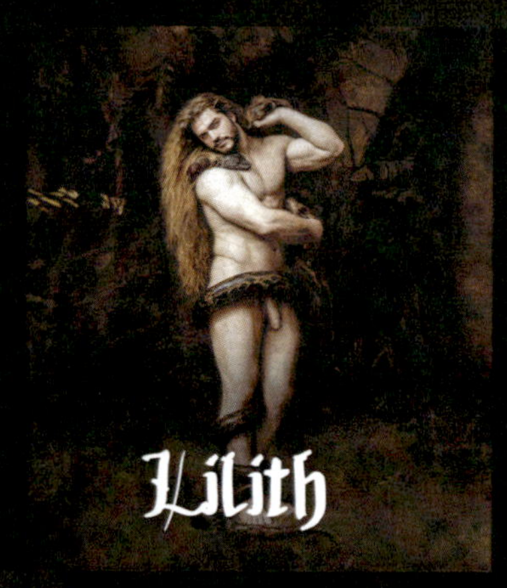

ASTRA ZERO REVAMP OF,
LILITH, BY JOHN COLLIER,
1887

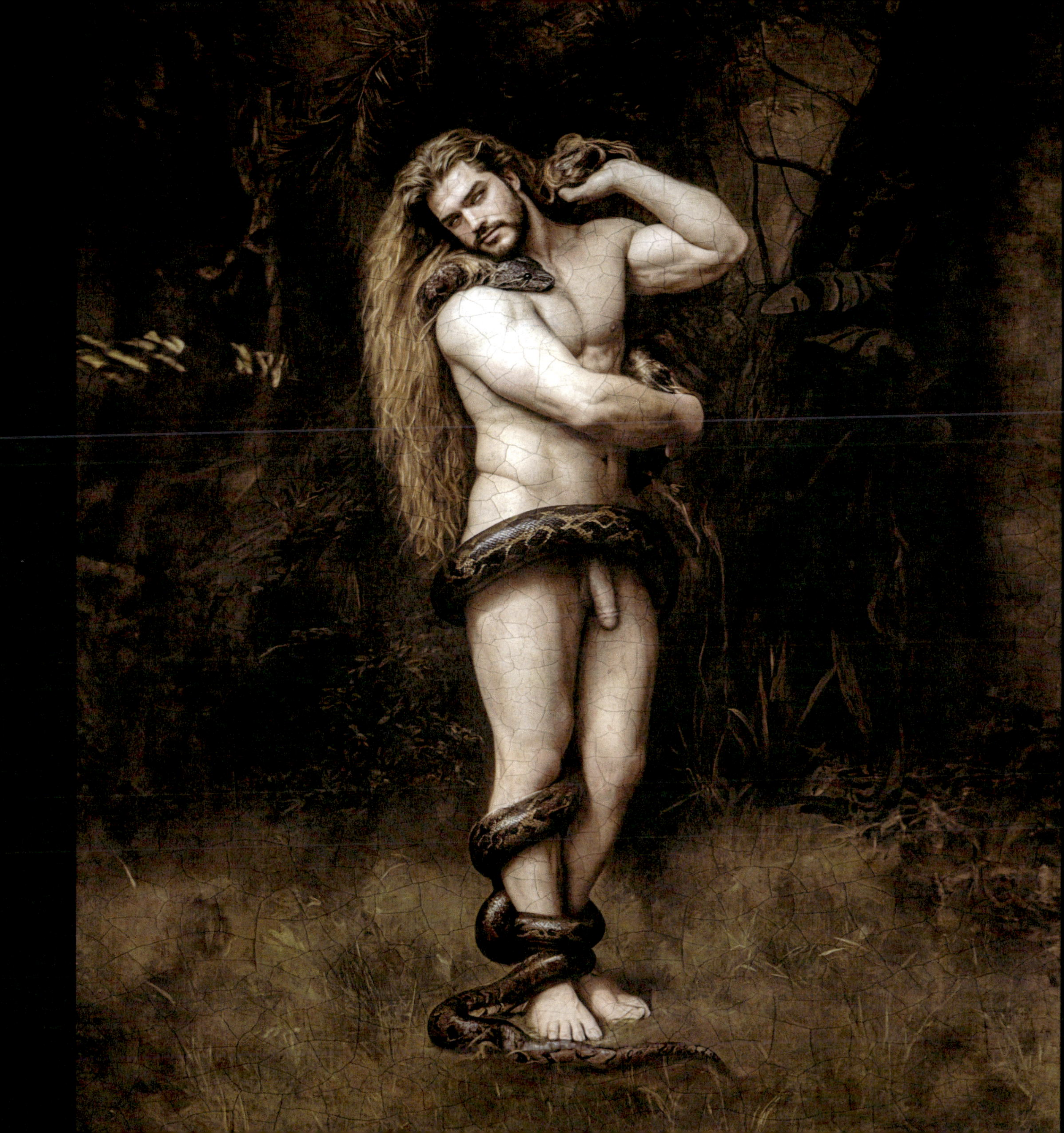

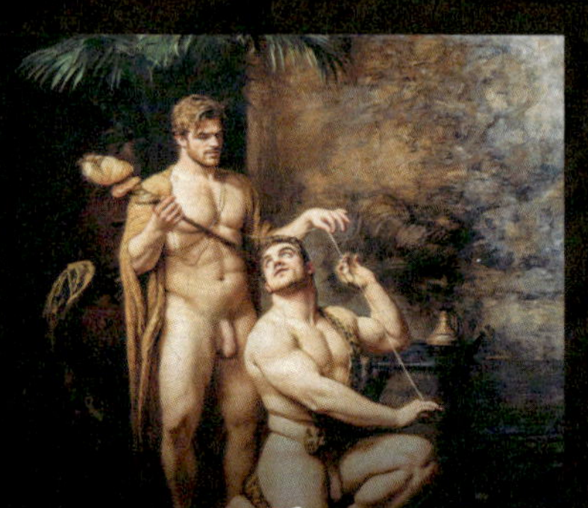

Hercules at the Feet of Omphale

ASTRA ZERO REVAMP OF,
HERCULES AT THE FEET OF OMPHALE,
BY GUSTAVE COURTOIS,
1912

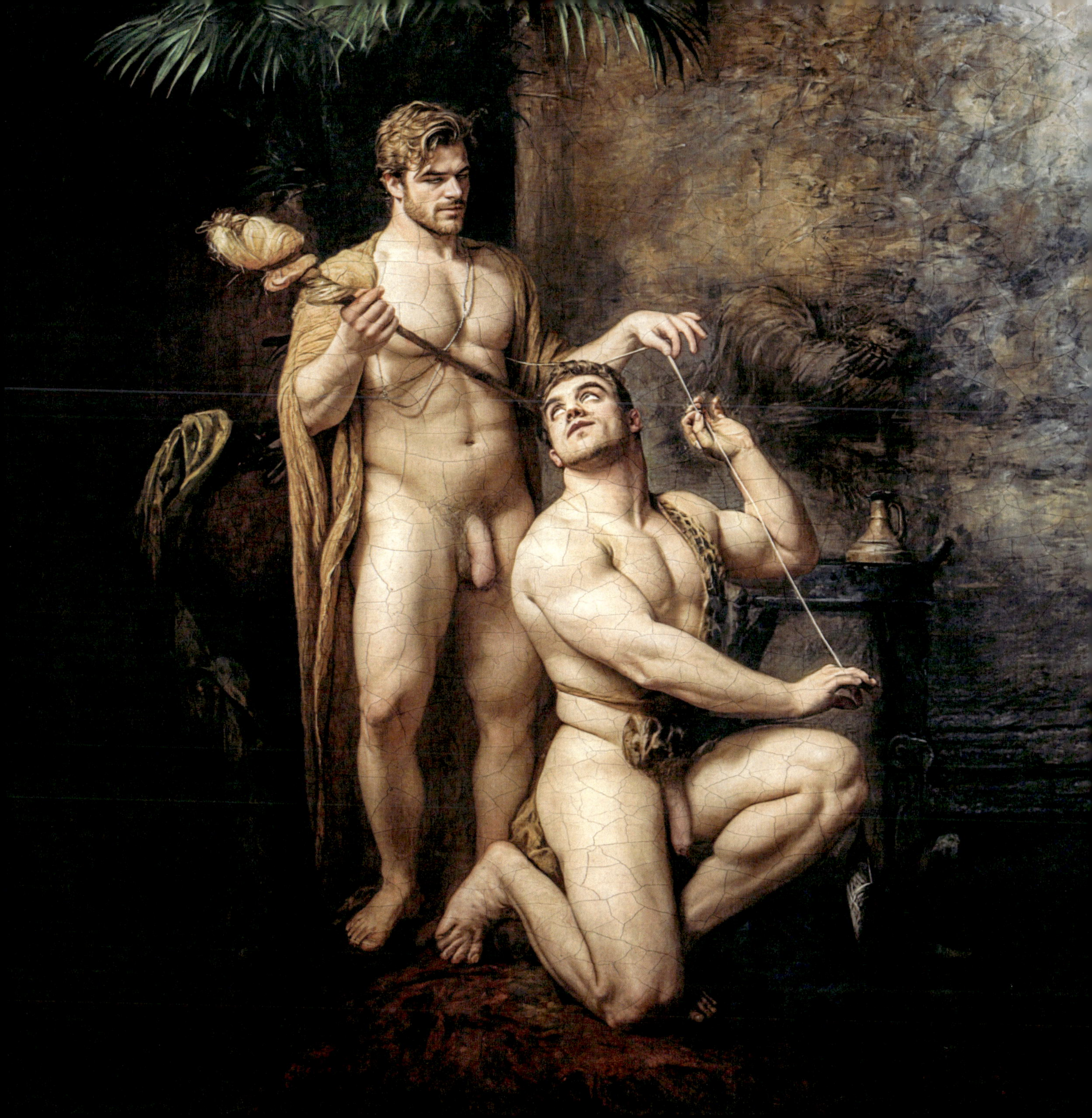

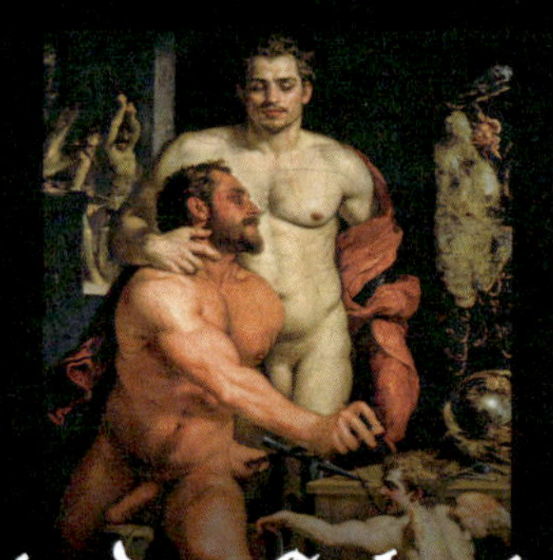

Venus in der Schmiede des Vulkan

ASTRA ZERO REVAMP OF, VENUS IN DER SCHMIEDE DES VULKAN, BY BARTHOLOMEUS SPRANGER, 1610

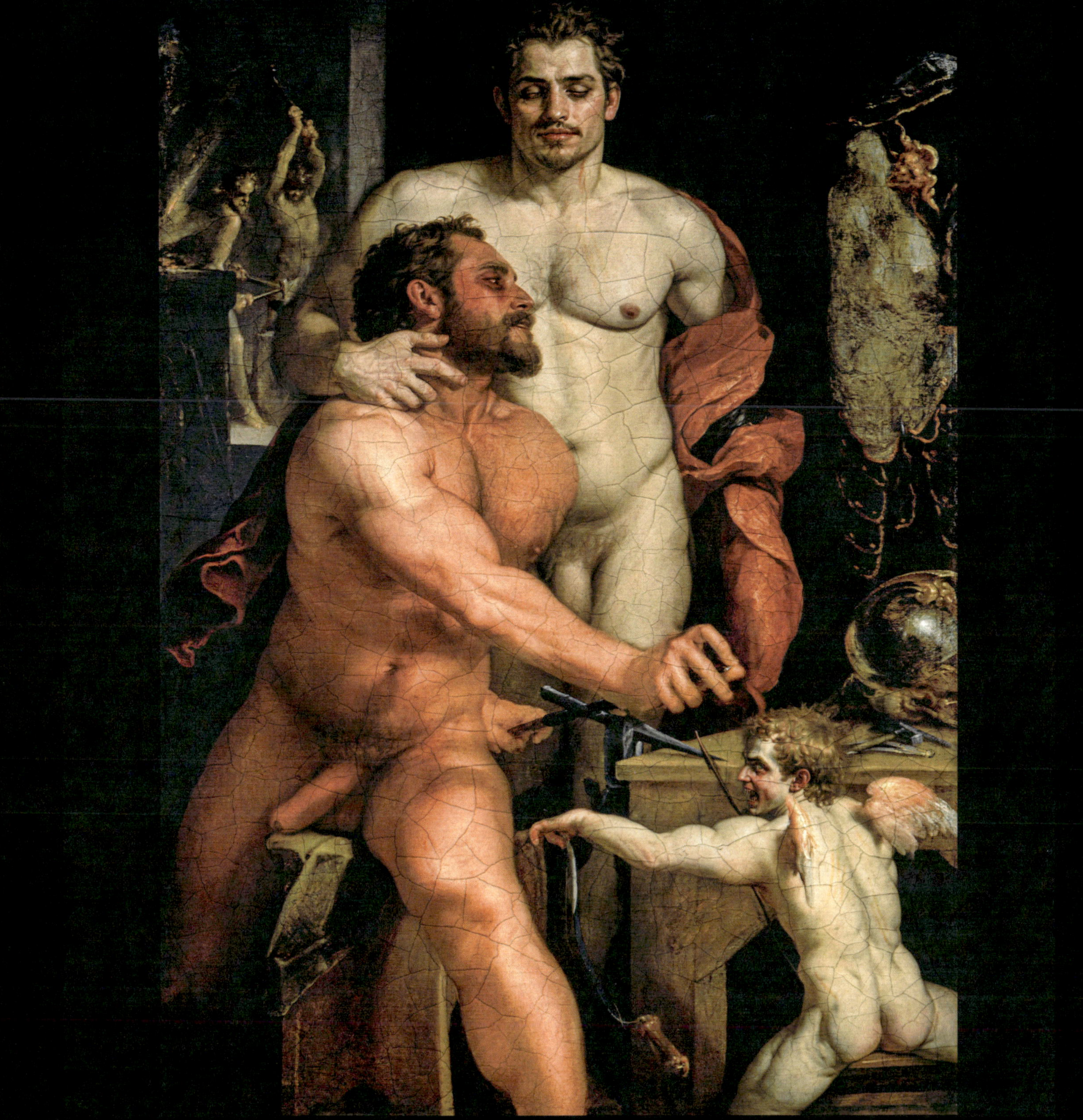

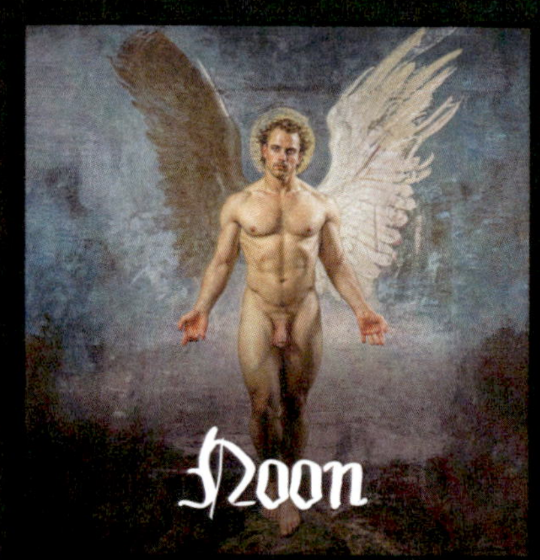

ASTRA ZERO REVAMP OF,
NOON, BY ABBOTT HANDERSON THAYER,
1921

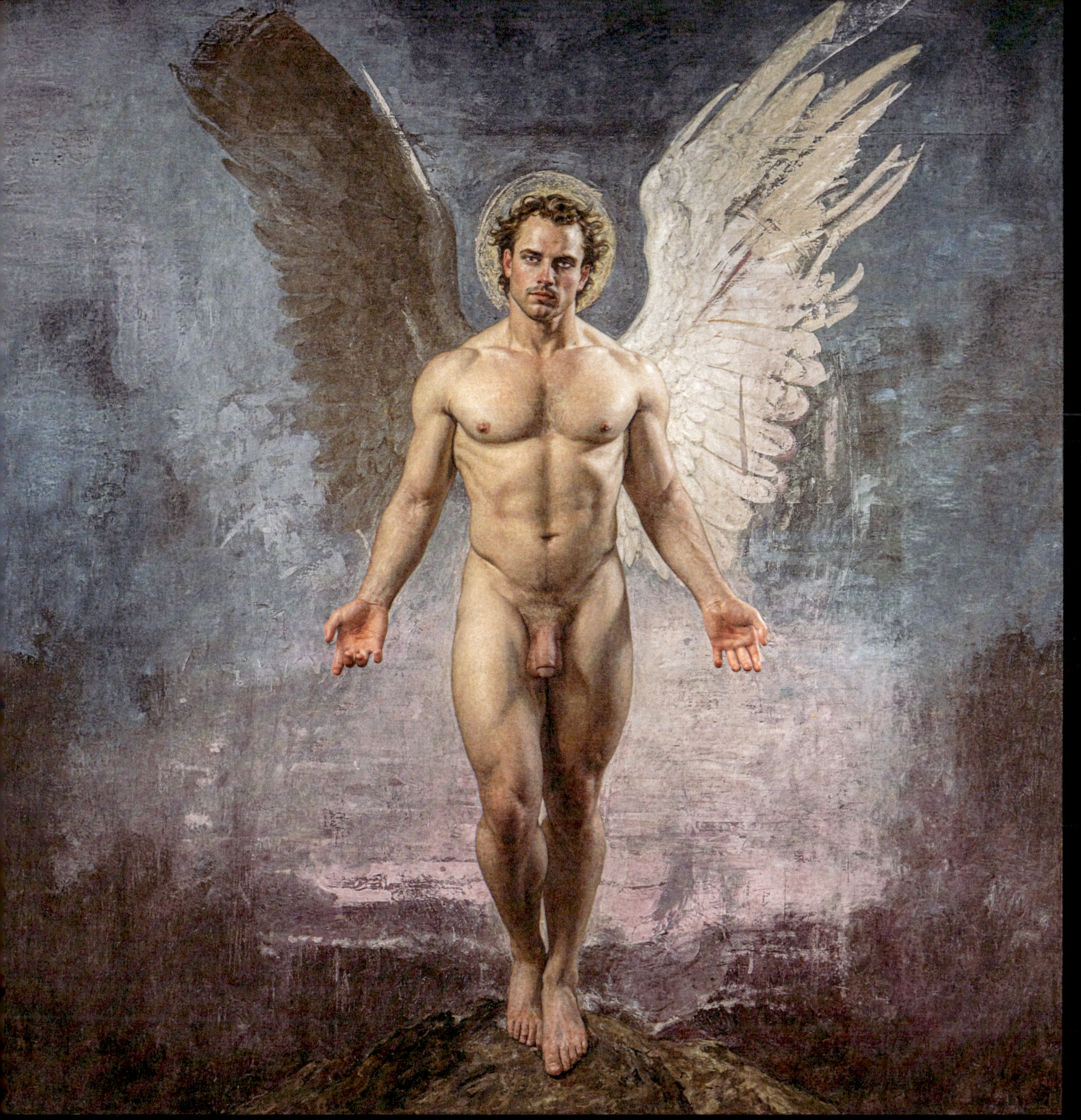

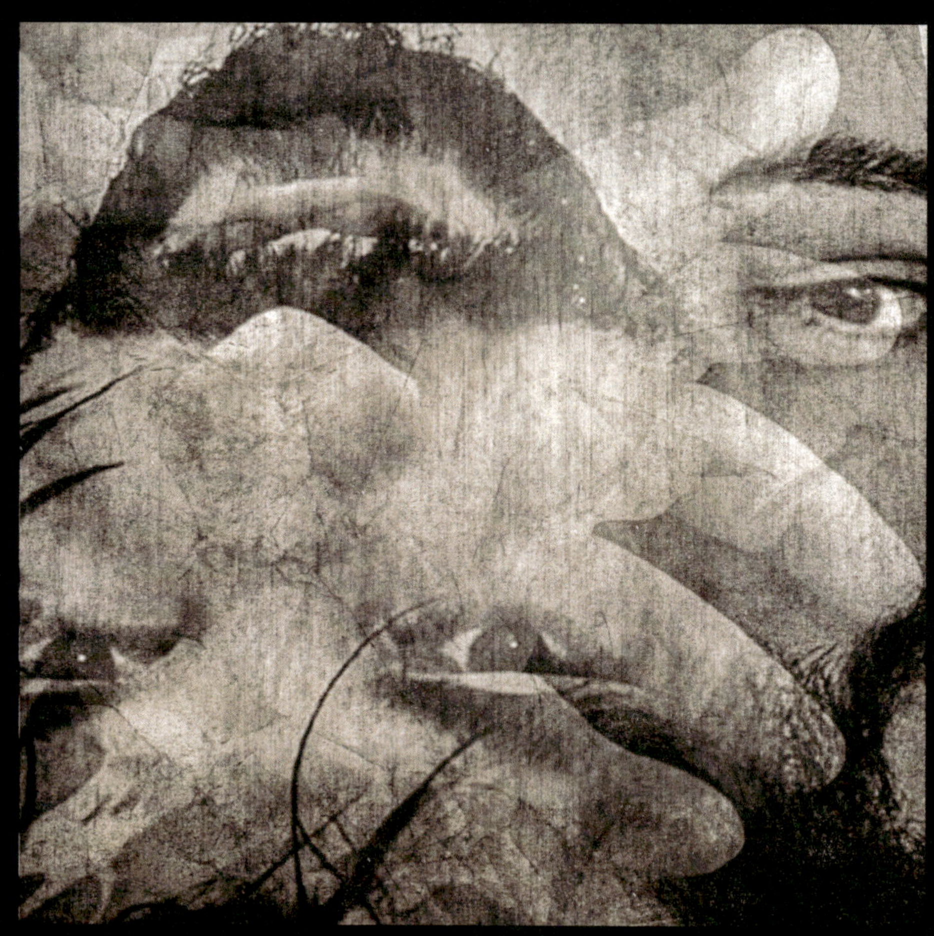

SELF PORTRAIT

About the Artist

Astra Zero (born Dustin Nicholls) is a queer Canadian alternative visual artist, designer, illustrator, video editor, creative director and songwriter.

His work fluctuates from a gothic macabre style and spooky cute themed visuals to his more popular sexually charged style of gay themed monsters, pop culture and historical revamped artwork with a dark erotic twist.

Starting off as a mainly 2D Artist with drawing & painting, His work has evolved to incorporate & mix more mediums and styles into his workflow, from Photography, 3D rendered work and digital painting, to animation, photo / video editing and graphic design.

You can see more of his work on social media @astrazero and on his website: www.astrazero.com